PASSED ON:
Public School Children
in Failing American Schools

PASSED ON:
*Public School Children
in Failing American Schools*

LOUISE MARR

NEW YORK

PASSED ON:
Public School Children in Failing American Schools

ISBN 978-1-61448-556-8 paperback
ISBN 978-1-61448-557-5 eBook
ISBN 978-1-61448-558-2 audio
Library of Congress Control Number: 2013935095

Morgan James Publishing
The Entrepreneurial Publisher
5 Penn Plaza, 23rd Floor,
New York City, New York 10001
(212) 655-5470 office • (516) 908-4496 fax
www.MorganJamesPublishing.com

Cover Design by:
Perla Marr
Rachel Lopez
www.r2cdesign.com

Interior Design by:
Bonnie Bushman
bonnie@caboodlegraphics.com

In an effort to support local communities, raise awareness and funds, Morgan James Publishing donates a percentage of all book sales for the life of each book to Habitat for Humanity Peninsula and Greater Williamsburg.

Get involved today, visit
www.MorganJamesBuilds.com.

Habitat
for Humanity®
Peninsula and
Greater Williamsburg
Building Partner

To my three amazing children, with love.

TABLE OF CONTENTS

DECEPTIONS AND MISCONCEPTIONS

The first time I got a sense that something was very wrong was in July 2010, on the last day of summer school at a high school in Philadelphia. I had just finished teaching a four-week session. I had turned in my final grades the day before, and this was the day that students came in to pick up their report cards. I was walking down the hall, when I heard someone yell to me from behind, "I passed, asshole!" I turned around and saw Rasheed[1], a student of mine. He was taunting me by holding up a copy of his report card as he walked away down the hall.

Most students take summer school classes because they failed the class during the regular school year. Each summer class is a roughly three and a half-week intensive course that is designed to cover the main topics in a very small amount of time, and students have the opportunity to make up the entire year in several weeks and receive a passing grade. Many students at this point are satisfied with a low "'D'" because they just want to move on, get the minimum credits, and leave high school behind. In order to pass, students have to complete class work, take a certain number of tests, and not miss more than two days. Rasheed had come to class almost every day during summer school.

But that was it, he came and did nothing. Based on his experience in public schools, he probably knew he could pass even based on "doing nothing." He was right.

Although absent on some test days, Rasheed would come to class on time almost every morning. Once class started, he would either wander around the room, talk back to me when I asked him to do his work, walk out of class randomly, or fall asleep at the back of the room. This was summer school; consequently, none of the discipline pieces that are set in place during the school year were available—no detention, no security guard to call when a student told you to "fuck off." I called his home several times, but was unable to get in touch with a parent. At this point in the game, a student has gotten himself into a last chance situation. He can pass the class he failed during the year, get the credit, and move on. If he blows this, he has to take the class over again during the school year. If he is a senior, this might be the class that prevents him from getting a diploma.

Rasheed probably did about 50 percent of his class work. There were four tests administered, he did not take one. He missed his midterm and the final. When it came time to calculate his grade, he had around 40 percent out of 100 percent. A "D" or passing grade is calculated at a 65 percent. I turned in an "F" for him to the office along with all of my other students' grades. What happened? The principal changed his grade to a passing one. He is free to move on to the next grade: all in the name of making "the numbers."

I was flabbergasted when I found out. As soon as Rasheed was out of sight, I went to see the Roster Chairperson, the person to whom I had turned in my grades, and who was responsible for recording them. I asked to see his grade record sheet. Not only had the 40 percent been changed to a 65 percent, someone had also changed the individual calculations (i.e., tests, class work, etc.) to add up to the final fictional percentage. I was shocked and angry that (1) an administrator had done this, and (2) the message we were sending to Rasheed and all the other students was "Do the bare minimum of work and you will pass anyway.

After all, we don't expect much from you." What would happen to a young adult who leaves high school thinking that this was how to get along in the world?

Teachers are scrutinized on their ability to engage students. We are expected to create rigorous and interesting lessons, define and implement clear and specific daily learning objectives, attend professional development classes, and make call after call to the parents of all misbehaving, failing and truant students. Yet, after a year of being evaluated on my abilities, attending mandatory sessions about how to engage students, make learning exciting, and how to accommodate all learners, in the end the principal could change the grades of the failing students at his or her discretion to save face and money. How will our students compete in the real world?

The numbers are carefully analyzed: the numbers of students graduating, percentages of students performing at a proficient level on state exams, and attendance percentages. Sometimes the principals have to make a few adjustments to hide large numbers of failures. What would be easier, failing these students, and making them repeat classes, possibly repeat a whole year, or just changing their grades to a passing one, and moving them out of the system? Of course it is easier to pass them on. After all, public schools do not have the resources to help a seventeen-year-old who can barely read. Who is this helping? It is helping the school budget. How does it affect the individual student? It puts them on a fast track to making poor choices. Take Rasheed for example, he received the credit for which he came to summer school. As far as he is concerned, a student can show up every day, do some work occasionally, and pass the class. He did not master any skills. He was not able to demonstrate proficiency in the subject. Yet he passed. He will most likely graduate from high school. He will probably not attend college, as this was never a goal of his. So he might find employment as an unskilled worker. Did he receive an education? Not really. He learned very little in his four years of secondary school. Did the school district serve this child? No. It was not prepared for him. It does not have the services that this student needs. Months later, I learned that Rasheed came from a very difficult family environment. He was homeless for a period of time, and at the time of summer school, he was living with a foster parent. He could have benefitted from therapy, working with a mentor or getting more individualized attention. I learned from some of the summer school teachers that Rasheed had a long history of behavioral problems at the school.

Students like Rasheed push teachers away, and make it difficult to make a connection with them. In Philadelphia, most students come from poverty stricken neighborhoods. There are many scenarios with failing students. Some are so insecure academically that they get involved in an endless cycle of behavioral problems that follow them throughout their school years. Some students come into a class and very early on, they recognize that the material is too difficult. They cling to the most comfortable coping mechanism they know—acting out. Instead of paying attention and doing the work, they start to cause problems; talking to other students, walking around the room, being loud, and talking out of turn. This will get attention from peers or even get them kicked out of class, and removed from an environment where they might have to perform. This might be the only way they know how to handle the stress of school. Many are years behind because they graduate year after year without mastering their subjects.

I teach grades 9-12, and large numbers of students in my classes in the last two years were below grade level readers. How did they reach high school without learning basic reading and math skills? After months of teaching in overcrowded classrooms to students who threaten to "fuck you up," students with emotional and behavioral problems, with no support for low skilled, or Special Education students; many teachers give up and allow them to graduate. In Philadelphia, the school system is set up so that unless a teacher can prove that he or she has provided endless interventions to help, a student must pass even if they have not fulfilled the requirements. In the Philadelphia School District, teachers are required to report the students' behavior, attendance, and academic shortcomings in a program called CSAP (Comprehensive Student Assistance Process). According to the school district website, the CSAP program is "a three-tiered, collaborative process by which schools identify barriers to learning and remove them by accessing internal (school-based) and external (community-based) resources."[2] In reality, it is an endless collection of paperwork documenting students' behavioral and academic problems. When I first came to the district and was introduced to CSAP, I was hopeful that once I reported the students' issues, a team of counselors would follow up with the appropriate support. Unfortunately, this doesn't happen, because there is no money. The paperwork just piles up, and gets put into neatly organized binders that get filed away.

If a teacher gives a student a failing grade, the teacher must provide the following: (1) evidence of all letters sent home to notify the parent of the failing grades, (2) evidence of multiple phone calls home, and (3) detailed documentation of interventions that the teacher has implemented to help the student (tutoring, longer time for testing, among other things) The process and the paperwork is very time consuming. During many report card periods, in addition to calculating passing grades, I have spent an extra six hours filling out all the paperwork to justify the failing grades. The students who failed my classes were students who never turned in homework, missed tests, were absent many days, and did no work. I have been in meetings with teachers and counselors, when the process is being explained to us and on more than one occasion, a teacher has leaned over and whispered, "I'm not doing all that work. It will not make a difference, even if you fail them, the principal can go in and change the grade anyway."

At the time I taught Rasheed, I had been teaching for one year in Philadelphia, and had eight years teaching experience in another state. After that day in summer school, I transferred to Vaux High School, a public high school in North Philadelphia, later taught at two other inner-city public schools, and my eyes opened up to many contradictions within the public school system. Too many times, we are letting students pass from one class to another, then from one grade to another without mastering the skills and requirements that are put forth by their very own school district. "Accountability" has become a popular word in educational reform. It is usually used to refer to teachers. What happened to the accountability of the student? I started to see a scary trend in the public schools. The principals are very focused on the "rating" that the superintendent gives them, because it is tied to not only funding, but also status (at least in Philadelphia, schools are categorized into groups that are based on achievement, state test scores, attendance, as well as other factors). There are high levels (top-level vanguard schools) to failing schools (identified as needing complete restructuring). Because of this, administrators will change students' grades to make the school look more successful. I have heard story after story of this happening in our school district. One teacher described a situation that involved a student who had failed a class. He took the class over for a second time. At the end of the quarter, when his teacher told the principal that once again, the student had not completed his work, had been absent for many days, and was going to fail the class a second time, the principal replied, "You can fail him if you want to, but as a principal, I will be overriding the grade, and changing it to a passing "D." Usually, the principal does not notify the teacher, the grade is just changed without anyone knowing.

As teachers, we must help our students prepare for the state tests, because they serve as our "report card" to the state. Requirements of President George W. Bush's No Child Left Behind Act of 2001 (NCLB) state that schools that want to avoid losing some of their annual budgets must show that their schools are improving year by year, made evident by standardized test scores. If they fail to make AYP (Annual Yearly Progress) for five years, they are identified as "failing," and run the risk of reconstitution under a restructuring plan. The state tests are so important, that at two of the schools where I have taught, staff members have driven to students' homes to bring them to school on the day of the test to make sure they take it. Every number is crucial.

Because of its poverty, high rates of violence, and millions of dollars of debt, the School District of Philadelphia is an extreme example of a school system in peril, and there is a lot to be learned from it. More than once, I have been told, "If you can teach in Philadelphia, you can teach anywhere." In the spring of 2011, the *Philadelphia Inquirer* published a series on the pervasive violence in Philly public schools. The following account tells a typical Philadelphia story:

> For Teshada Herring, the action was unmistakable: The girls smearing Vaseline on their faces and fitting scarves to their heads were preparing for a fight. The ritual—well-known in Philadelphia schools—is intended to keep skin from scarring and hair from getting ripped out. As Teshada passed the group on her way to class at Audenried High that morning, the events of the previous week flashed through her mind—a fight she had witnessed, Facebook posts warning that someone from her neighborhood would be attacked, a text blast to her phone that all but named her as the intended victim. She wondered: Would they come for her? Minutes later, while taking an algebra test, Teshada was unable to stop thinking about the pack of girls. She glanced up from the test, looking at the classroom door. The girls in scarves passed by. Teshada was terrified; now she was sure they were coming for her. Suddenly, a band of more than a dozen girls and boys— captured on video roaming the halls and looking into classrooms—barged through the door. The group converged on Teshada and began to beat her. In less than a minute, they vanished. "It was like a tornado," her teacher would later say. "They went one way, then they went the other way.[3]

This excerpt describes a situation that many Philadelphia teachers are familiar with. In fact, after spending time in Philadelphia schools, both teachers and students become numb to the violence and the anger. All day long, as teachers, we hear nasty, crude insults hurled at teachers and students alike. I am sure that many people would run from Philadelphia schools if they got a glimpse of what teachers deal with every day.

In *Passed On*, I would like to shed some light on the conditions of our schools to demonstrate the need for change in our education system. Today, in 2012, millions of dollars are being spent on school reform. The push is towards giving students and parents a choice in education. In the past ten years, we have seen many programs surface such as: vouchers, charter schools, and cyber schools. However, many of these ideas do not even begin to address the issues that we see in failing inner-city schools. Philadelphia is a great example of how our education system has forgotten and ignored poor children.

I strongly disagree with the corporate reformers of today, who seek to hold teachers responsible for our failing public educational system, and promote the privatization of our public school system. "If only we could get better teachers!" they say. "If only we could put a 'master teacher' in every school! If only we could weed out the bad teachers!" Most of these reformers have little to no experience teaching in failing schools, yet they propose to get rid of educators, and employ illogical evaluation systems that will be tied to student test scores. Their focus is dangerously misdirected. I taught for eight years on the West Coast, in a city that differs in many ways from Philadelphia, Pennsylvania. It has been in the last three years that I have become acutely aware of the inequities in our schools. There is a huge disconnect between corporate reformists' ideas for solutions and the reality of the inner city classrooms, and an unjust trend to privatize our public schools, while totally ignoring the students' physical and mental health issues that impede learning.

Great teachers leave the profession every year because of the horrendous working conditions, and the disrespectful manner in which principals treat them. Educators are very aware of what they and their students need to succeed. Yet, many administrators do not consider teachers as professionals or as valuable resources. I am not an expert on education. However, I do have eleven years experience in the public school system, and feel strongly that there is a need for more honest discussions about what is happening in our public schools. The loudest voices we hear today about educational reform are those of wealthy corporate reformers who do not have a real understanding of what thwarts the progress of students in underperforming schools. In addition, it is clear that in the name of "improving schools," there are many entrepreneurs looking to make money from the failing education system, through creating charter schools, online schools, and other services. Their motives are clearly monetary; not to help underprivileged children succeed.

Some educational reformers, for instance Bill Gates, are investing millions of dollars in educational research and programs, while at the same time ignoring the facts that huge numbers of failing schools are in poor urban settings. Poverty, though many believe should not be considered an obstacle for a child's success, does affect a students' ability to learn in the classroom. If we do not openly and honestly address this extremely influential factor, we cannot make effective changes. Without putting support programs in place to help these poor children become better students, we are not going to make progress. Many of the ideas presented by corporate reformers relate to improving the quality of our teachers. What reformers do not understand is that additional programs are needed inside the schools to support them. The problems in each classroom are too overwhelming for one teacher to tackle. The effects of poverty spill into our schools all day long. Because of high poverty rates, there is a huge need for more Special Education, counseling, and mental health programs to supplement classroom learning. Most of the reformers today come from wealthy privileged homes, and cannot begin to understand what these children go through on a daily basis, and how it affects their ability to perform in school. Too many reformers insist on using teachers as the scapegoats for all of the education system's ills, and it is time to look more thoroughly at what we are up against.

Many reformists, including Gates and U.S. Secretary of Education Arne Duncan, propose new teacher evaluation systems that will remove incompetent teachers and reward teachers who produce higher test scores. If teachers were given a work environment with the support and tools needed to succeed, this might make more sense. Unfortunately, that is not the case. In our Philadelphia inner-city schools, where most failing schools are located, our classrooms have anywhere from 30-50 percent special needs children. (Even though the School District of Philadelphia reported the number of Special Education students as 11 percent last year, I am referring to my actual classes.) In the last two years, in two of my classes, the number of Special Education students started out in September around 30 percent, and by March, it had risen to 50 percent, as new kids transferred in from other schools.

These are students with emotional, behavioral, or learning issues. They are integrated into general education classes in the "inclusion model," that is supposed to benefit students, when in actuality, it puts both students and teachers in an impossible situation. In one eleventh grade class of twenty-eight students, for example, there might be nine students who read at anywhere from a first to eighth grade level. Teachers are expected to teach to all levels at once, which is exceptionally problematic. General education teachers are not trained to work with extreme behavioral problems, children who read at low reading levels, or kids who have just gotten out of jail. Most college educational programs don't offer courses in how to deal with these issues, yet critics are quick to judge teachers as "bad" if they cannot produce an increase in test scores in these conditions.

These students have very specific needs that are not being met. It happens first in the elementary schools, and children continue to move on to the next grade without having mastered basic skills. Principals push to graduate them. What happens next? They end up in failing middle schools, then failing high schools. Our values have become so compromised, and our system has become so lax, that students receive a diploma without receiving a real education. These are the classrooms in which teachers are expected to raise test scores.

In the past year, both presidential candidates Mitt Romney and President Barack Obama visited Philadelphia high schools, but neither visited a failing school. Obama went to two of the top public schools in our city (Masterman and the Science Leadership Academy), where test scores are high, and students are doing well. These schools are "special admit" schools; in other words, students have to possess a certain grade point average to get in. This is a poor representation of what is happening in most of our city schools. Regular public schools must admit all neighborhood students who walk in the door, and cannot remove students with extreme behavioral problems. Both Obama and Romney needed to see firsthand what is going on in these schools. Instead of just analyzing data, policy makers should visit the classrooms and talk to the teachers. Most public high school teachers work with anywhere from 100–120 students a day. We educate, work with, talk to, listen to, and discipline them. We know what tools are missing from our job; we know which out-dated systems in the district actually work against us. We know where money could be spent more effectively. How can there be such blindness on the part of reformists, policymakers, and politicians? The vagueness and inaccuracy in their statements about our educational system is shocking.

I wished that either of the presidential candidates would have spent a day in an inner city classroom, not just given a speech on graduation day, or met with the founder of a charter school. I doubt either would have lasted until lunchtime. Romney did visit a charter school in the city, but did not set foot into the schools representing the majority of our students' experiences, the inner city public schools. His comments at the charter school to his audience of a few teachers, administrators, and the founder of the school clearly demonstrated a lack of knowledge of our education system. For example, Romney told them that his team had analyzed results at schools in 351 cities and towns in his home state and found no correlation between the number of students in a classroom and performance. When discussing the study, he stated, "As a matter of fact, the district with the smallest classrooms, Cambridge, had students performing in the bottom 10 percent," Romney told the group. "So just getting smaller classrooms didn't seem to be the key."

Ask any experienced teacher in any subject if class size makes a difference. It is a no-brainer. Smaller classes help students to get more individualized attention, which results in higher achievement. I wondered if Obama and Romney were afraid to step past the doors of the inner city schools, as both went to college preparatory high schools. It can be a little scary and overwhelming at times. Many students have parents who are in jail, or are addicted to drugs. They grow up in violent neighborhoods. A huge number of kids (from ages fourteen to eighteen) are parents themselves, participating in a never-ending cycle of teen pregnancy, dependence on welfare, and dropping out of high school. Students might have heckled the presidential candidates—they have no problem threatening teachers, and they are accustomed to using violence to solve problems. But why look the other way? These are the young people spilling into our workforce, they are undereducated and unprepared.

Much like the corporate reformers, Romney's white paper on education, "A Chance for Every Child," proposed that it is the teachers' unions and the teachers who are at fault. "Teachers' unions are consistently on the frontline fighting against initiatives to attract and retain the best teachers, measure performance, provide accountability or offer choices to parents."[4] If unions and some teachers seem to be opposed to providing choices, it is based on the opinion that giving charter schools money drains funds away from public schools that serve the poor. Most teachers would agree that the union is not our enemy, as many politicians want the public to believe. They might not always be as effective as they could be, but the union is often the only protection we have in a corrupt, dysfunctional system that allows principals and administrators to unfairly treat teachers. If a teacher is too outspoken, it is very common for a principal to fabricate stories or poor evaluations to be able to move them out of the building. The union is our only recourse in these situations. This has happened in every school that I have worked in. At each of the turnaround schools (schools that were forced to undergo restructuring because of poor test scores) where I have taught in Philadelphia, at least three teachers announced at the end of the year that they were leaving teaching altogether. Some had worked in the private sector and were appalled at how we were treated as educators.

Philadelphia has a large number of troubled schools; in other words, schools that are located in ghetto neighborhoods where truancy is high and violence in the classroom is common. When I first accepted a position at a turnaround school, I spoke to several teachers who said they would never transfer to one, because they knew that the violence and stress levels were so high. This coming from teachers who already worked in troubled schools. Last year at my high school, three teachers went on extended health leave owing to stress, anxiety, or panic attacks. I also know of at least four teachers who were taking antianxiety medication each morning, mostly due to the violent, erratic behavior of the students, and lack of support from the administration that compounded the negative work environment. Somehow though, politicians think that we can just "get rid of bad teachers," and get a whole crop of new ones. Good luck. Doesn't it make more sense to utilize the talent we have, give help to teachers who need it, and provide a more stable learning environment for the students? For the past two years, in late spring it breaks my heart when even the most difficult student asks, "Are you leaving in June too?" These kids have very little stability in their lives as it is. Even principals don't seem to understand the importance of consistency in developing a positive institution of learning. They are so caught up in punishing and retaliating against teachers who speak up with new ideas, that they would rather exercise their power to get rid of a teacher than to work on nurturing a collaborative and cooperative environment for teachers and students.

In the 2012 campaign, both of our presidential candidates promoted charter schools as an alternative to public schools, and spoke of the importance of giving parents a choice of schools. In the past few years, there has been some documented success in charter schools in inner-city environments. What some people fail to realize though is that most charter schools have the ability to manipulate the population of students through lotteries, excluding special needs children, and expelling aggressive students with emotional problems. This difference is huge. They end up working with a different population of children. There are many bright students in our inner-city schools, but this segment of the population is underserved. These very smart, thoughtful, and capable students get lost in the chaos. With so much time and energy spent on the challenging students, who literally yell out for attention and often make it impossible to learn, these students fall behind and get sucked into an environment of apathy, distrust, and rebellion.

The idea of giving people choices about their education is a reasonable one. The problem with applying the concept of choice to the public educational system is this: charter schools will end up serving the talented and motivated of poor children, whose parents have the initiative to research options for their children. The other talented students without parental support will become the apathetic ones, and the students with special needs will stay in the public schools as an only option, and continue to be underserved. Opponents of charter schools fear this very scenario, and ask the question, "What will happen to the public schools who serve the poor children who are left behind?"

When presidential candidate Romney discussed the huge achievement gap between white students and students of color, he said, "This unconscionable reality flows as a direct consequence from the poor quality of the schools that serve disproportionately minority communities in low income areas."[5] Instead of funding these schools to provide them with a better education, many propose to close them and give up. Is the achievement gap due to bad schools in low-income areas, or is it because Black and Hispanic students are often raised in poverty, exposed to violence at a young age and are too unhealthy and traumatized to learn? Creating other schools will offer a choice to some, but will leave many more in failing schools.

Why not invest this money into the existing public schools? Many of the parents of these children do not care about choice. This sounds harsh, but the reality is that there are a huge number of children in these schools who are dealing with drug addiction in the family, unemployment, or family members in jail. These parents do not answer the phone when teachers call home to discuss issues with their child. Often their phone is disconnected or they have changed numbers, and in nine months never bother to call the school to update it. These parents *cannot* and *do not* research choices for their children. Many of our students don't even live with their parents. They live in foster homes, at a homeless shelter, on their aunt's couch, or at a friend's house. Who will choose for these children? Most likely no one, so they will end up at an underfunded neighborhood public school. We may create choices, but these students will be unable to make one. Who will choose for these children? Who will be the voice for those who cannot speak for themselves?

As a public school teacher, I am deeply concerned that the public, including parents and students going into teaching and public policy programs, has no idea about what is actually going on in our public schools today. The most dominant opinions we hear today are those of the corporate reformers, who have the power and millions to make sweeping changes to our school system with little to no accountability to parents, teachers and students. These changes are being made at the federal as well as the district level. The message that parents continuously hear is that because of the unions and the poor quality of teachers, our schools are failing, and the best solution is to close public schools and replace them with privately run schools, such as charters and online schools. By writing this book, I hope that more people will understand the struggles our schools and teachers face today to educate our children. As much as corporate reformers want the public to believe otherwise, teachers care deeply about their students' successes.

With this book, I hope to give the public a glimpse into the public school classroom. It is my hope that *Passed On* might spark a more honest discussion about where we need to focus our energy in order to make effective changes in our American Public Schools. My eleven years as a teacher have been in five different high schools, and only two states. My experience might be very different from a teacher in Montana or Nevada, but I have read enough from teachers across the country to know that we share many common issues in our classrooms, and our goals are the same: to provide all of our public school children with an equal access to a quality education that will prepare them for a productive life. Whether they choose to go to college or not, teachers want our children to be able to make educated, thoughtful decisions for themselves in order to make positive and productive contributions to our society.

Chapter One

VAUX HIGH SCHOOL: "TURNAROUND TO GREATNESS"

A twenty-minute bus ride from Center City, Vaux High School is located in a poor north Philly neighborhood. Row houses line the streets; abandoned homes with boarded windows sit on almost every block. On the corners, there are what Philadelphians refer to as "mami and papi stores," small bodegas run by Puerto Rican families, which sell candy, lunchmeat, sodas, cookies, chips, and canned goods. It is futile to try to find anything healthy in these little stores. Most of the Vaux students stop here to get breakfast in the morning on the way to school: a soda, a bag of chips, and some candy. The contents are dropped into small black plastic bags that are used by all of the bodegas, and the empty bags are found all over the school.

Built in the early 1900s, the old, brick school building takes up one square block. The cleaning staff once told me that in the summer months, if you were out on the sidewalk in the early evening, you could see streams of bats coming out of the chimney. During the school year, the principal had to be called to the fourth floor more than once to kill bats that were flying around in classrooms. One of the students' favorite stories was about the time he killed one with a baseball bat. Also sharing the building were mice and flying roaches.

The projects are two blocks away, and many of the Vaux students live there. This is a neighborhood school, and except for a few who ride public transportation, most students walk to school each morning. Although, most kids live only a few blocks away, getting students to come to school on time at 8:00 in the morning was one of the yearlong problems. If you taught a first period class, you could expect half of your class to arrive anywhere from thirty to forty-five minutes late. Some didn't arrive until 10:00 AM. Calls were made home and detentions were written. It is very difficult to change a culture and an attitude towards education. This is ingrained in the history of the neighborhood.

Students would make jokes about not living past the age of twenty-one. The drug trade is prevalent in this area of the city. Everyone is familiar with it, or knows someone who is involved. Many of the students at the school have parents who are addicts, incarcerated, or related to someone who is. One morning early in the year, I overheard a group of my students comparing how many times their dads had been shot, "My dad has been shot here, here, and here." Nija said, as she pointed to different parts of her body. Nine months later, her sixteen-year-old cousin would have to hole up in his house for a week because he was afraid of being shot by an enemy. A few of the parents of the successful students did not let their children go outside after school. This was the only way to completely protect them from the violence.

In 2008, Arlene Ackerman was hired as superintendent of the Philadelphia School District, and soon after, she proposed her five-year reform plan, "Imagine 2014, Imagine Greatness." This was in response to President Bush's NCLB, which proclaimed that all students would be proficient in reading and math by the year 2014.

NCLB changed accountability systems and placed more emphasis on testing and analyzing data with the intent of creating better programs for students. The annual evaluation of schools is an important piece of NCLB. Schools must make AYP (Annual Yearly Progress) toward the state goals, or suffer consequences. AYP is the minimum level of progress that schools must achieve each year on annual tests and other assessments. Parents whose children are attending Title I (low-income) schools that do not make AYP over a period of years are given options to transfer their child to another school or obtain additional educational services. After a school misses the AYP target for a fourth consecutive year, the school is required to take "corrective action," which could involve replacing teachers and staff. After five years of a school's inability to make AYP, the school could be completely restructured.

Parts of Superintendent Ackerman's plan included closing the city's worst performing schools, and reopening them as "Renaissance Schools." Under the umbrella of the Renaissance Schools, she created the "Promise Academies," which were turnaround schools under her direct supervision. In March of 2010, the district identified five schools to be completely restructured under her management: two elementary, one middle, and two high schools, of which Vaux was one. The plan was implemented relatively quickly. It was announced that no more than 50 percent of the existing teachers in these schools could be rehired . If they wanted to stay, they would have to interview for the position along with the other applicants. Interviewing began in the late spring, and when it was over, ten teachers stayed on at the school, and twenty-two new ones, including myself, were hired.

"School turnaround—this adrenaline-charged moment that we are presently in—is about rapid and dramatic improvement not just in test scores but also in culture, attitude, and student aspirations," explains Laura Pappano in her book *Inside School Turnarounds*. [6] That we can even propose to make dramatic change in such a short periods of time is far from realistic and puts schools in a precarious position. Years of systemic dysfunction in any form cannot be changed in a year or two. Unfortunately, because of the way that the system is set up, where districts have to be in competition to get funding, shortcuts will be taken, and honesty falls by the wayside. We need to find sustainable solutions. One of the problems that people buy into is the idea that schools can be "turned around" in a one to two year period. Careers of superintendents and principals are often on the line, and too many people want to see numbers increase quickly.

School districts want to improve test scores and student aspirations. But, as we discussed in the introduction, in failing schools, there are students who have been in under-performing school environments for years and they have little to no support at home. They are accustomed to a school system that encourages the "passing on" of students who do minimal work. In a high school, it is a huge undertaking for one teacher to bring up test scores when children are so far behind. Students who have attended failing neighborhood schools their entire school career have learned how *not* to work hard. At the end of the quarter, many students fail because they either don't come to class, don't come on test days, or never do any work. These students should receive failing grades, but even if they do, they know that they can take a six-week credit recovery class, or just take the class over in the summer, so why bother now?

In Philadelphia, several harmful crutches encourage laziness and lack of accountability on the part of the students. Specifically, summer school (a three and a half week course to make up an entire year); credit recovery (an after school six week course to make up an entire year's worth of work); and an understaffed Special Education Department (SPED), that allows all kids in the SPED program, whether they have a mild or severe learning disability, to pass whether they complete any work or not. These crutches set kids up for failure. In fact, on several occasions, when I asked a student why he was not doing his work, he replied, "I'm just gonna take the class in summer school." This was in January, and he planned to just sit in class and do nothing until June.

Changing the culture and attitude of the students is one of the big pushes in turnaround schools. Principals try to change the environment of the school, hoping that students will start to take education seriously and leave behind everything that they have felt about their entire educational career to this point. As the system is structured now, it is extremely difficult to affect change on the family and neighborhood culture outside of the schools. Our principal at Vaux tried to get more parents to come up to the school and become more involved, by having a jazz band play at the teacher/parent night, and by starting a weekly "lunch with the principal," open to any parent who wanted to come. Few parents took advantage of this, and attendance was poor. Change of this nature—trying to get parents in poor neighborhoods to become involved in their kid's schooling is a difficult task. Parents are struggling with other things in their lives, and do not take the time to support their kids. Maybe they are working, or maybe they are not accustomed to being involved. But, over and over, we were disappointed by poor parent turnout anytime we invited parents to come to the school.

It's hard to have sustainable results when schools have no money to support the programs. In the spring after our first year of the Promise Academy, the district announced huge cutbacks and layoffs and the school fell apart. Even the principal, who was so "committed to the kids," left to go to another school (he reportedly received a hefty signing bonus). In May, when the students started hearing about the layoffs and budget cuts, many were understandably upset. Students had found advocates in their teachers and then learned that the teacher could not stay because they were being laid off. Many of these kids were Special Education students, and they were sad about losing their caseworkers, who had supported and guided them the whole year.

"This is a turnaround. Whether we close a school, open a new one, or fire the principal and hire a new staff, the point is that schools must now engage students differently."[7] This is a common belief among educators, that we must find new ways to get students interested in learning. So, we now have smart boards, laptop carts and computer labs, and teachers are evaluated on how well they are engaging students. Teachers spend hours and hours on the weekend planning classes, creating presentations, and designing ways for students to discover the information on their own through projects and activities and research projects. However, if certain problems are not addressed such as: lack of parental involvement, lack of funding for SPED students, no support systems in the school for emotional and behavioral problems and kids living in extreme poverty, then an exciting class means nothing. If a child comes to school in the morning, and cannot stop thinking about the fact that his parent is in jail, or using drugs, or does not know where he will sleep that night, he will not be able to focus on the lesson, no matter how engaging. For those of us who have not grown up in similar environments of poverty, the closest example I can present is this: imagine trying to watch an exciting movie in the theater, but you are too sick to enjoy it. You are feeling so feverish or in pain, that you cannot concentrate on the movie. You need to get medicine for the ailment first. Schools need to address these issues that affect our kids living in poverty first, and invest money into programs that are accessible to the kids every day.

When a school announces to the staff that it will go through the turnaround process, usually teachers are notified that they can interview to stay if they want. This can be unsettling for students as well as teachers. One of the English teachers at Vaux who had interviewed to come back to work there, learned at the beginning of the new year that she had lost all of her senior classes to a Teach For America (TFA) teacher (a teacher with no experience), and was going to be teaching several remedial reading classes a day. By staying at Vaux, she was demonstrating a commitment to the school. In fact, she had made the decision to stay because of several students that she cared a lot about. On the one hand, teachers do have to get used to getting their schedules changed on a whim of a principal, but just like in all professions, employees would like to believe that as years pass, that they will be rewarded with certain recognition. At Vaux, eight of the teachers were from the TFA program, which allows college students to teach in the inner city without having completed a certification process.

The TFA teachers were committed, hard working, and contributed a lot to the school. Many people are critical of this program because the TFA teachers do not have an educational background, and often end up teaching subjects for which they do not have a certification. Frequently,

TFA teachers leave education when their two-year commitment is up. In a school such as Vaux, which has such a large number of disadvantaged students, it is important not to discount the value of building relationships with them. You cannot put a number or a statistic on this piece. Many of these kids do not have close relationships with adults, and to have someone at school to trust, to help guide them, advise them and encourage them is crucial. Whether they admit it or not, students desire consistency in their lives. This all falls apart when in June, teachers leave, get laid off or are replaced because of restructuring. This problem is common in troubled schools. As Anthony Cody, teacher and educational advocate, explains about his school in Oakland, California, "Our problem is not how to get rid of people—it is how to retain them. Most of our vacancies are now filled by interns who have received a crash course in the summer. They struggle to learn the ropes the first year, and by the end of their second year are becoming effective. The trouble is 75 percent of them leave by the end of their third year. Our mentoring program has made a difference, but we still struggle to retain people, especially those recruited for a two-year commitment. Our pay is low, conditions are challenging, and the emphasis on test scores makes it even harder to keep our teachers."[8]

The next September, a new crop of teachers shows up, and it takes months to build trust with the students. Just when a teacher feels like the relationship is working with a student, bad news comes at the end of the year. This is very common in Philadelphia, where many teachers change schools every one to two years.

Because 30 percent of the population of the Vaux High School was in the Special Education program, we had a team of seven Special Education teachers and an SEL (Special Education Liaison.) One of the new programs at the Promise Academy was team teaching. In the majority of the classes, there were two teachers, cutting the student to teacher ratio, and helping with classroom management. This was a huge learning curve for many teachers, who were used to working alone. However, they worked enthusiastically with a common purpose and embraced the challenge. In some of the classes, such as the world languages, art and technology, the teachers taught alone.

In addition to the team teaching model, another of the unique qualities of the Promise Academy was the longer number of hours students were in school: an extended day until 4:00 PM, Saturday school every other week, and an additional three weeks in July. Some studies have shown that more hours in the classroom can improve student performance. This was part of Ackerman's push for excellence. Teachers signed a two-year contract to work for the additional twenty-eight hours a month and an extended year. Teachers also had a common planning time, where we met in committees for an hour each day, in addition to our individual hour of lesson planning time.

The extended day model was problematic from the start. The Promise Academy schools failed to find a constructive way to use the extra time. Students complained about having to stay until 4:00 PM. Originally, the extra hour at the end of the day was designed to be an hour of enrichment. Students could choose from a list of classes; drama, music, dance, cooking, and archery were a few of the classes offered and taught by the teachers and staff. Unfortunately, many kids just wanted to go home, and after awhile, as soon as the bell rang to signal the end of the sixth period, the school police, principal, and any available staff ran to staff the doors, because kids would walk out in droves.

For part of the year, a woman from the Salvation Army taught the cooking class during the enrichment hour. Her full time job was teaching cooking to ex-cons transitioning into the workforce. During the class, which was held in the school kitchen, she had to continuously reprimand the students because they constantly tried to steal food from the refrigerator and cupboards. Regarding their disrespectful behavior towards her, she said, "I teach ex-cons and I can't believe how much worse these kids are." She quit after a few months. Every other Saturday, kids were expected to come to Saturday school, which was held from 9:00 AM to 1:00 PM. Unfortunately, the administration had a difficult time deciding what to do on these Saturdays; whether to tutor, offer more enrichment, or regular classes. Because the law only requires students to attend 180 days of school, there was no way to enforce Saturday school. We were told by the principal to tell the kids that it was "required," but not "mandatory." The kids saw right through this, and most stayed home. Attendance for Saturday school hovered around 30 percent all year.

Many of the students at Vaux had attended schools in the neighborhood all of their lives. Two of the teachers had been at the school for over twenty-three years, and they had taught some of our students' siblings years ago. Contrary to the public's perception however, this is a rarity; gone are the days when teachers stay at the same schools for years and years. Especially in the urban schools, teacher turnover is high, due to difficult working conditions and budget cuts. Teaching in urban failing schools means teaching to a poor community, in which many people do not value education. There are some families who want their children to do well in school, but trying to get the parents to support your efforts is an arduous undertaking. It is hard to get the kids to see a connection between a high school education and life after graduating. Many view school as a necessary evil, something you must do, but that has little value. They want results fast; they are used to communicating through instant text messages: when you press a button, you get an immediate result. Studying and reading take too much time, and you have to wait too long to see a return. A frequent response from students when I would hand out an assignment, even to write a short paragraph was "This is too much!" In addition, few role models in the families and community can demonstrate success in school and career. Because of poverty, methods of obtaining money quickly are more favorable, such as drug dealing and receiving public assistance checks.

At the beginning of the year in my advisory class, I started a discussion about options after high school. A common exercise in high schools is to have the kids work up a budget for living on one's own. I worked with the class to add up all of the expenses that an adult is responsible for: rent, utilities, food, phone, et cetera. We then calculated the monthly salary of a worker at McDonalds, so they could see the value of a higher paying job that could be obtained with an education. Brianna blurted out, "Well, my sister does fine and she has two kids and works at McDonalds. She has money for food and all her bills." Then she added, "Well, she do live in a Section 8 house, so her rent is low." Unfortunately, the attitude is "It's good enough." There is little incentive for many children in poverty to improve their lives. Many of my students accepted that their lives would always be in North Philly, and they had a hard time seeing beyond it. As Jay McCleod explains about his experience working with children in poverty, "Several decades of quantitative sociological research have demonstrated that the social class in which one was born has a massive influence on where one will end up. Although mobility between classes does take place, the overall structure of class relations from generation to the next remains largely unchanged. Quantitative mobility studies can establish the extent of this pattern of social reproduction, but they have difficulty demonstrating how the pattern comes into being or is sustained. Leveled aspirations are a powerful mechanism by which class inequality is reproduced from one generation to the next." [9]We try as educators to expose the students to other cultures, ideas, and opportunities outside of their neighborhoods and city. But for many, it is extremely difficult to visualize beyond the neighborhood.

The teachers who came to work at Vaux were an exceptional group. In addition to the new teachers, many of the improvements to the school in the beginning of the year were visual: the principal spent a decent portion of the school money to repaint, and to refinish the floors and stairways. As in any business, difficult decisions have to be made when it comes to the budget. Some teachers were confused when the principal announced he was spending thousands of dollars to buy plastic plants for the front hallway, when many of us didn't have a full set of textbooks. The only supplies we were given were two reams of copy paper per month (this is standard for schools in Philadelphia). Teachers buy pencils, (students rarely brought writing utensils to class), pens, chalk, rulers, books, construction paper, printers, posters, and any other needed supplies. A handful of teachers received computers, but most of us had to bring our own laptops to school. If you wanted to do a special project that required supplies, you had to buy it on your own. After teaching for a while, you get to the point where you just accept this. Imagine a cook being hired by a restaurant, but told he has to bring his own pots, pans, knives, and ingredients. However, the truth is that there are more pressing matters to be concerned with. During one meeting at the beginning of the year, when a teacher raised her hand to ask when the copy machine would be fixed, the principal made a comment about how we all needed to learn to do without, and then said to us, "I could teach in the middle of Cambodia with a stick and a rock!" That was our favorite joke for the rest of the year, especially while waiting in line to make copies, "What's the matter with you, you can't teach with a stick and a rock?"

When the principal announced his fake plant purchase, this was probably the first time the teachers got a sense that we were putting on a show for the superintendent. The Promise Academies were new, so it would take time to be able to analyze data and measure progress. We needed at least a full year to make any kind of comparisons. The state tests, Pennsylvania System of School Assessments (PSSAs), would be an indication, but the tests were given in March, and results don't come until the end of the year. This is why the teachers were surprised when we were shown a video in December that was used to promote the Promise Academies to the public. In the video, there were graphs showing improvements in test scores. We looked at each other in disbelief and wondered, "How can they be showing progress so fast, where did these numbers come from?" It had only been three months. It was apparent that the administration was working hard to demonstrate progress, at the cost of honesty. The pressure to show improvement is so high, that administrators fabricate it. Funding, bonuses and reputations are all on the line.

Some system had to be established to evaluate the ongoing progress of the school. Attendance, number of suspensions, and the number of violent incidents were all part of the evaluation. The Promise Academy management team came up with the "walk through" as a way to monitor consistency and compliance with the standards of the Promise Academy way. Formal walk-throughs occurred every four weeks or so. A group of educators from the school district offices would come to the school, break up into groups of two, and walk around visiting the classrooms. They came in with clipboards, observed the classes, and took notes. We were evaluated on classroom management, student engagement, teaching methods, and lesson plans, among other criteria. A significant part of the evaluation was focused on the visual environment of the classroom, such as clearly visible learning objectives, vocabulary lists, and student work. Papers on the wall are tangible and could be counted, whether a student understood a lesson or not was harder to measure in a snap shot visit.

The principal and vice-principal also took turns doing their own ten-minute observations. We would receive feedback in our mailboxes the next day. According to district policy for all schools, unless tenured, all teachers are supposed to receive two formal observations a year. Aside from the observations, the principal was not directly involved with teaching, unless there was a specific problem, such as a grade change. Especially at the Promise Academy, the principal was very busy with the promotion of the school, and the maintenance of good public relations.

As part of the "Promise Academy Way," all teachers had been given a list of things that we were required to have on our class walls, as well as a revolving display of student work in the outside hallway. The goal was to have uniformity in the classrooms. But many teachers commented that the students never read the required labels on our blackboards; they existed more for the administrators' viewing pleasure. The day after a walk through, teachers were informed if we had been rated "green" (the highest rating), "yellow" (good, but room for improvement), or "red" (reason for concern). That was the end of the dialog. There was a short conversation with the principal to reveal the color you had earned, but no discussion of a plan to help teachers to improve. It would be more helpful if there transpired a process to assist teachers to improve in specific areas of concern.

Every four weeks or so, as I walked into the building in the morning, the waxed floors were a sign that we were having visitors that day. The principal chose his favorite students to represent the school, hiding the troublemakers in the in-house detention room on the first floor for a few hours. Because the Promise Academies were the superintendent's "pet project," principals and students from other schools, politicians, and reporters came to check us out. To the teachers, it felt like there was a huge effort on the part of the administration to project a positive image, and it was not completely truthful. One day during a visit, the teachers noticed that the bells had not rung to signal the end of class. Ten minutes, then fifteen minutes went by until they finally rang. Later, we found out that the principal had told the office to hold the bells until he had all of his visitors safely inside the auditorium. He did not want the visitors to see how the kids really acted at Vaux. They most likely would have heard nonstop yelling and cursing and maybe a fight or two. He could not risk projecting a negative image. This was just one of the many things the principal hid from the public. In a March 29, 2011 guest blog for the School District of Philadelphia, our principal wrote, "Roberts Vaux High School has spent years listed as a persistently dangerous school due to confirmed arrests for robbery, rape and aggravated assault. In the 2009-2010 school year, Roberts Vaux accumulated (28) dangerous incidents. This year, the Promise Academy at Roberts Vaux High School has had (0) dangerous incidents. These efforts can also be seen in the 50 percent decrease in the number of violent incidents (mutual confrontations) that have occurred among students."[10]

Schools are not only judged by the test scores, they are also rated on attendance, number of suspensions, and number of "dangerous incidents." Our school police told us that he was very upset because the principal instructed him not to report the many serious incidents we had at our school. The principal had told him on numerous occasions *not* to fill out a report on dangerous incidents, and there was nothing he could do about it. The few I knew about that weren't reported were the robbery of eight laptops by a student, two incidents of weapons brought by students, and two arrests for drugs. We all felt duped. The problem that many principals do not understand is that when they are dishonest in representing our school, as well as dishonest to the teachers and staff about what is happening behind the scenes, they lose the respect and support of everyone. I have seen this happen in all of the public schools where I have worked. It was inevitable that many teachers lost confidence in the principal as soon as they saw the veil of dishonesty.

Teachers need support especially in areas that are unique to failing schools, such as dealing with behavior or emotional issues. For example, if it is observed that a teacher needs help with classroom management, the district should require the teacher to attend seminars on this specific issue, and then follow up to make sure changes are being made in the classroom. There must be collaboration and trust between teachers and administrators. Too often, the relationship is an antagonistic one; working against student progress. If more effort were spent on a collaborative effort between administration and teachers, all parties involved, especially the students would benefit. Schools need in-house teacher coaching and support. Unfortunately, there is rarely money in the budget for this. It is difficult to break through the punitive environment that exists in many public schools.

Many principals prefer a dictatorship style of leadership, and within a few short months, the communication between principal and teachers breaks down. This results in unhappy and frustrated teachers, many who have to fear retaliation from the principal. If a principal is dissatisfied with a teacher, or even in cases of personality clashes, principals will go after them by writing them up for small infractions, resulting in a conference with the union. Time, energy, and stress wasted on these petty meetings could be used in more productive professional training time. Many reformers today believe that teachers should be let go if they are not "great" teachers. Why not fund additional training and coaching for those teaching professionals instead of giving up on them? Many critics minimize the challenges of teaching. If someone has invested time and schooling because they are passionate about teaching, it is counterproductive to discard them and hire someone with no experience, especially considering the time lost in the first year as a novice. Considering the high burnout rate with teachers in public schools, it would be more productive to work towards a more supportive work environment, and to nurture talent instead of treating them as disposable. The district does offer some professional development seminars for teachers, but they are primarily for accruing required continuing education credits. Administrators would see more improvement in teacher performance if they required specific courses that were focused on issues that apply to helping disadvantaged children.

Teaching in a poor urban school is much more complicated than just bringing up test scores. Many of these students have such traumatic living situations that they are very slow to trust other people. In any school, successful teachers are the ones who can build relationships with students. In an inner city school, it is even more crucial because so many other factors just are not there (such as parent involvement, high expectations for work ethic, or respect for education), and gaining trust and respect often takes longer. In a suburban school, or a school represented by higher income families, most students come to school with the value of education they have learned from their families and community. This value is often absent in failing schools. In an inner-city school, most public school teachers don't come from the same socioeconomic background as their students. Those who do, have an advantage because they have a better understanding of what the kids go through every day. Teachers who have only read about poverty in books most likely go through a period of adjustment when they realize that their students' experiences are so different from their own. There are often multiple barriers a teacher has to break through before a student is even open to learning.

One of the many challenges in inner-city schools is the fact that there is little to no parental involvement. On teacher/parent night, out of my 120 students, six parents showed up. When I asked William, one of my students if his mom was coming that night, he replied,

"No, I don't think so."

"Why, does she have to work?" I asked.

"No, she's home watching TV, we live right across the street. She is just lazy." Many kids come from one-parent homes, but it's not always because they are working that they don't get involved. There is an attitude that education is the teacher's job. Many parents don't respect education, or acknowledge its importance, and this message is loud and clear to their children. These are the attitudes that are part of the underperforming school culture, and they take time to turn around.

Very few parents have e-mail, so the two modes of communication that teachers have with parents are by phone or letter. When a teacher has problems with a student, we are expected to make contact with the parents. Sometimes an administrator will arrange for a parent to come to school for a conference. On three occasions over the course of the year, the dean of students arranged for parents to come up to see me about their child who was having issues in my class. One day in December, Ty's mother came to my classroom to speak to me because he had been acting up in class every day, and refusing to work. His mother stood in front of me as I explained to her how her son did very little work, was disruptive, and disrespectful to me. When I finished, she turned to him and said, "What I want to do is punch you in the face, but it's too close to Christmas and I don't want to go to jail." Needless to say, there was no improvement in his behavior. He failed the year, and made the class up in summer school in June.

Violence is a common way to solve problems in North Philly. Students grow up in an environment where threats are an everyday occurrence. When I first started at Vaux, I wasn't used to having fifteen year old girls say to me, "Shut up, or I will slap the shit out of you!" But after a few months, you almost become numb to the violent verbal exchanges. From eight in the morning to four in the afternoon, we heard nonstop violent, aggressive cursing in the halls, in the classrooms, and on the streets. In fact, these young students are so accustomed to this environment that they are always on the defensive and are very distrusting. In any school, the first year is always the toughest for teachers because it takes time to build relationships with students so that they accept your help. At Vaux, this problem was magnified because the students were quick to assume the worst of people, and to dismiss things that were out of their comfort zone. It was as if they felt they had to be able to fight back at all times. This was true of even the girls, who had no fear of physical violence themselves, and would even invite it at the slightest provocation. As one teacher said that year, "These kids are in crisis, they can't learn in this state. They face the crisis of poverty, of dysfunctional families, drug addiction, and incarceration. They shut themselves down to learning." It is easy to stand on the outside as many wealthy reformers do today, and comment, "Poverty doesn't affect learning, all kids can learn." Unfortunately, it is not that simple.

A large percentage of the students at Vaux had children of their own. The boys who fathered children were anywhere from fourteen- to eighteen-years-old. As a teacher, I would overhear them talking about their girlfriends and kids. Many of these young boys had no interest in being involved in their children's lives. As illustrated in Elijah Anderson's book *Code of the Street*, boys with promises of love lure young girls. "When the girls submit, they often end up pregnant and abandoned. However, for many such girls who have few other perceivable options, motherhood, accidental, or otherwise, becomes a rite of passage to adulthood. One of the reasons for this may be the strong fundamentalist religious orientation of many poor blacks, which emphasizes the role of fate in life. If something happens, it happens; if something was meant to be, then let it be, and "God will find a way."[11]

The Elect Program was established by the district to help student parents. It is housed in the school and the counselors help the young mothers with schoolwork, parenting, day care and other services. Early in the year I found out that my student, Penelope was pregnant and she later gave birth to her baby in May at the age of sixteen. She was a good student, but she started to miss a lot of classes. After she told me she was pregnant, she suddenly had a lot of doctor or midwife appointments. She would take off entire days to go to one appointment. I saw her working with the counselors in the Elect Program, but as the year went on, she missed more and more school. She would come in sporadically for make-up work. She told me that she wanted to go to nursing school one day. She was a smart girl, and if her attendance were better, I am sure she could have received straight "As." She made a special effort to complete her projects, and she created some beautiful work. Unfortunately, she missed too many days and work to receive higher than a "C." The number of pregnant girls at our school was staggering. In every class, I had at least two girls who were either pregnant or had children. One day, one of our teachers spoke out about the Elect program. "I am against it. We are making it easier for them to have kids as teenagers. We are just sending the wrong message." On the one hand, you want to help these young girls to complete their education. On the other hand, with services in place to help young mothers, students see fewer disadvantages to having a baby, and take no precautions to prevent it.

I found it interesting that we had a program that helped young mothers and fathers in the schools, yet we did not provide information about sex or pregnancy. With little guidance at home, girls at age fourteen do not make the best decisions when it comes to their sexual health.

In Philadelphia, according to 2010 city data and 2009 stats from the Centers for Disease Control and Prevention (CDC): "The rates of gonorrhea and Chlamydia infections of youth between age fifteen and nineteen are respectively, four and six times higher than the citywide average. And 15 percent of all births in the city (of Philadelphia) in 2008 were to mothers age nineteen and younger."[12] There is no curriculum for sex education in the district. Our health teachers did present a unit on reproduction this year, but this was for high school students. By this time, it is often too late for many of these kids. They are sexually curious, open to new experiences, and slow to think things through. It would make more sense to offer sexual education at much younger age, so that kids can make educated decisions. It is well known that teen parents struggle in school. They have a higher number of absences, fail more classes and many end up dropping out. In one year, four of my students dropped out of school to have their babies, or to care for their infants. The most common reason for absences is not having someone to care for the child. Teen pregnancy is more common among the poor, and compared to a middle class community, there is much less of a stigma attached to it. Poor young pregnant girls are not afraid of being labeled as failures, as girls in the suburbs might be. In fact, there is an attitude from many of the girls that they deserve to be treated as adults because they have a child. One day in second period, Tyneshia yelled at me, "You can't tell me what to do, I have two children!" Tyneshia was sixteen.

Penelope's sister, Roberta was a few years older than her. Roberta told me in the fall, "I dropped out last year because my mother died, then my aunt died and I couldn't handle it. But I am back to finish because I care about my future." Roberta was eighteen and a sophomore. She had been living with her dad, but they didn't get along so she moved in with her older boyfriend. She had three other sisters who all had children. In September, Roberta told me that she and Penelope no longer spoke because of an argument, but by the time she gave birth, they had smoothed things out. She also told me that Penelope's baby daddy was a good guy and that she had been with him since she was twelve and he was eighteen. I remember once that year when Penelope was telling me about her pregnancy, and she referred to the "baby in my stomach," and I realized how little she knew about what was physically happening to her during her pregnancy. Penelope took an incomplete for spring quarter to have the baby. Her sister, Roberta worked hard for the first part of the year, and then in the spring she dropped out again.

During an after school discussion with some of my female students that revolved around someone who was pregnant, I asked why more girls didn't go to Planned Parenthood for contraception. "What's Planned Parenthood?" Roneisha asked. According to the *Philadelphia City Paper*, "Pennsylvania law requires schools to teach students only HIV/AIDS prevention, but it does not spell out what that means and does not mandate teaching condom use." One teacher interviewed said, "They gave me the health class. They told me there was no curriculum for it and to just make it up. I have no experience in that field at all, and I asked the kids what they wanted to learn about. And they had so many questions about sexual everything because there was no sex education. So I ended up teaching it for half the year. But I wasn't required to do it," the teacher said. "If they didn't have me, they wouldn't have had it at all."[13]

Danielle was a freshman with one child, and her sister, Brianna was a senior with two. They lived one block away from school. Danielle was in my second period class. She was a husky girl, and she could easily pass as a twenty-year-old. She came regularly at the beginning of the year, and then her attendance started to wane. She made no secret of her disgust with school. On the days that she came, she would walk in and turn her desk so that her back faced the blackboard. When I was writing something on the board, I would say, "Danielle, why don't you turn around so you can see?" "No, I'm good," she would say.

When I asked her to do her work, a frequent response was, "Get outta my fucking face." Then she would miss the next four days of school. She did not pass the year in my class. One day in the spring, I was walking to the bus stop, and I came upon Danielle and Brianna sitting on their stoop, eating sandwiches. I said hello, then asked about their kids. "Oh, they're in school." I later asked another teacher how their kids could be in school, because I assumed they were too young. The teacher replied, "Oh, they meant daycare. Welfare pays for their kids to go to daycare, but the girls just stay at home." The government gives them each a monthly check to live on, and in addition pays for their children to go to a day care, but the girls stay home and don't go to school. The public assistance program seems to perpetuate teenage pregnancy by making it easy for these girls to drop out of school. To get some extra income, poor, unwed, nonworking mothers often let a relative or friend claim their child at tax time, the relative takes a few hundred for themselves for the favor, and the mother collects some cash. In school, I overheard many conversations about this in January and February, as the young moms were waiting for their tax money.

Alexis was seventeen, a senior and lived in the projects with her mom. She had a one-year-old daughter. The father of her child had been shot and killed the previous year, so her mom took care of her daughter while Alexis was in school. Alexis was very smart, soft spoken and mature for her age. When it was prom time, she told me she couldn't afford to go. She was upset about her living situation; she wasn't getting along with her mom and she had to wait to turn eighteen before she could apply for Section 8 housing by herself. She wanted to be a hair stylist. I would have loved to see her continue her education because she was hard working and focused. At the end of the year, she had too much to deal with to look into colleges. She told me that once she got her living situation settled, she might try the next year. Schools desperately need counseling services for these young girls. Too many bright, young girls are not equipped with the information to make sound decisions. Add to that the fact that many grow up without a father, and are desperate to find someone to love them, and think that getting pregnant will bring lasting happiness.

Tyreek had a difficult time in my class that year. He made a decision early on that he didn't want to work. He was disruptive in my class, and rarely lifted a pencil. In the fall, he was locked up for awhile, so he missed a week of school. When in class, he bored easily, so he would talk to his friends loudly and defiantly. I had to have him removed from class several times. One time after removing him, the dean of students told his mother that she was required to come to see me if he wanted to get back into my class. She came the next day. After I told Tyreek's mom about his refusal to work, she turned to him and said, "Come on, just get a 'D,' wouldja? Just pass the class." I told them both that I wanted him to work harder and that I had much higher expectations for him. I tried to get his mother to support me in telling her son that he could do much more. I let them know that I was available for tutoring anytime. She continued to say that a "D" was all she expected of him.

Tyreek failed the year. I saw him the first few days of summer school, then he stopped coming. The last time I saw him, I was walking to catch the bus on a Friday. A couple of cop cars were speeding down the street. They stopped at the corner before my bus stop. There were many people hanging outside on the sidewalks. Three more cop cars swooped in, apparently there was a fight. As I was walking past the corner, some teenage girls were yelling at each other. I saw Tyreek sitting with a friend on a stoop, watching the scene. When I got to school on Monday, I found out that Tyreek had been shot the night before four times: three in the back and one in the back of the head. The girl he was with was shot, too. They were both in the hospital. He was doing relatively well, but she was in a coma. I hoped Tyreek would recover, but unless he would move from the neighborhood, the disagreement between the shooter and Tyreek would probably not go away.

In February of 2011, Arlene Ackerman announced that our school district was in danger of a $400 million dollar deficit. It was threatening to be the largest layoff of teachers in two decades. Teachers were nervous and there was an air of uncertainty, as reports came out with new numbers every week. We were told that up to 1,000 teachers could be force-transferred, and many more laid off. In the end, the Promise Academy team-teaching model would only last one year, as it was obvious that the school district could not afford to maintain two teachers in the classrooms. By the spring, the atmosphere in the school was very different. Teachers were all talking about the fear of being laid off, students were asking us whether we were leaving, and it was difficult for everyone to stay focused when we all knew that the school was falling apart. We had started the year with so much hope, but we all felt duped. Sadly, many started to refer to the school as "The Broken Promise Academy."

By June, as the district tried to determine which Promise Academy teachers were safe from layoffs, many of us interviewed for other schools in the city.

Many of us lost our jobs, but were rehired in the fall. The school would re-open in September under the same name, the Promise Academy at Vaux High School. Unfortunately, almost all of the elements of the school that made it unique were gone: no more Saturday school, the four extended days were reduced to three and there would only be one teacher in each classroom. The only thing that was different from the school of two years prior was the name, which had now become a sad joke.

Chapter Two

POVERTY AND VIOLENCE
IN PUBLIC SCHOOLS

n an interview in June 2011 with U.S. Secretary of Education Arne
Duncan, he discussed his respect for Dr. Martin Luther King, and
said, "Martin Luther King is my big hero. When Martin Luther
King came to Chicago in '66, he pointed out the slum conditions
on the west side. Subsequent to his visit, tons and tons of money
went into that community for job training programs and all kinds
of things. But when I took over the Chicago schools in 2001, thirty-
five years later, the overwhelming majority were still desperately poor.
What became clear to me was kids were poor because their families
were poor, and families were poor because the quality of education
in that community hadn't changed at all. Ultimately, for me, the way
you end cycles of poverty is through educational opportunity. I draw
the line back to what I saw, felt, and experienced in Chicago, and
forward to national implications. If you don't change the quality of
education, you can't get out of so many of our social ills. If you do
change the quality of education, then you have a real chance to break
through."[14] How does one define "quality?" Arne Duncan defines it
solely based on the teacher.

Duncan's sentiment about wanting to give poor families access to a great education is shared by all teachers. The problem with his statement is that he implies that all we have to do is to put a new school filled with wonderful teachers into a poor neighborhood, and we can expect an automatic change. Poor children come to school every day loaded with the stresses of poverty-little to no food in the kitchen cupboards, parents addicted to drugs, parents dealing drugs, brother in jail, mother in jail, best friend just got shot and killed last night, 14-year-old girls getting pregnant, students living in foster homes, and the list goes on and on. These are all true stories from my own students in the past three years in inner city Philadelphia. These students need more than access to great teachers. Contrary to what many corporate reformers want the public to believe, it is a fallacy that inner city schools are filled with low quality teachers. In the poor neighborhood schools where I have taught, the teachers are caring, dedicated, and talented. However, resources are scarce, and support systems are inadequate to nonexistent. If a child comes to school with fear, anger, and emotional and physical pain every day, one great teacher cannot make it all go away.

The effects of poverty are felt every day in classrooms of inner-city schools. Children in failing schools have very different needs from students who come from stable households. We are wasting precious time trying to teach kids of poverty using the same methods used in middle class schools. Many of these children have violent tendencies, anger management problems and Oppositional Defiant Disorder (which is believed to often be related to having an alcoholic father or family member in jail) or other serious issues that not only affect the individual's ability to learn, but also negatively affect the other students in the class.

In inner-city schools, there are a lot of pressures to rebel against school. For many, this is a relief, because if you are in the eleventh grade, and cannot read past the second grade, at least you have peer support if you want to act out and not try. What is the alternative for the children who are up to nine years behind their grade level? For many students, they have been labeled as Special Education students for years. They know that they have fewer responsibilities than the other students do, and that with a bare minimum of work, they will pass. What is the incentive to try any harder? In a community of family and friends where most people around them have only a high school education, obtaining a high school diploma is often seen as the only goal-and they know it is very easy to attain. Public Schools who serve poor neighborhoods have become so lax, that students have learned to be underachievers. Children and parents have both been let off the hook, so generation after generation performs at a low level.

It has been my experience that there are students in failing schools who are capable of rising above all the chaos and performing well in these environments. It has also been my experience that these particular children have parents who are very involved in their lives and education. In failing schools in poor neighborhoods, these parents are the exception. Marcus and Richard, students of mine, were twin brothers who attended the same neighborhood high school in North Philly. They were both very focused, and worked harder than most of the kids in their classes. In a failing school, with 30–50 percent Special Education students per class, it is extremely hard to concentrate. It takes a special strength to be able to block out all of the disruptions (such as fights in the classrooms and teachers stopping the lesson to deal with outbursts from other students). Trying to learn and to be a good student in the environment of a failing school can be extremely challenging because there are so many factors working against you. Marcus and Richard had supportive parents who lived together in the same household. Their parents were among the few who showed up for parent/teacher night in September. The boys had encouragement at home and their parents set high expectations for them. They made sure their children did their homework, and they instilled a work ethic in their children at home. Students like Marcus and Richard risk being bullied, because they do not participate in the crazy behavior that is common for many of the other students. They must work hard not to get caught up in the negativity that exists in poor urban schools. They must be especially strong to be able to function in this environment, but somehow they do it. Many students cannot. Instead, some give in to what other students are doing: rebelling against authority, refusing to work, and wasting time in school.

Edward was a senior when I taught at Vaux. He also worked very hard; he was among the few students who would show up every day, even when there was a substitute, which is the day when most kids would cut class. He was always prepared, worked diligently in class, and had been accepted into college for the fall. I remember when he told me that he couldn't wait to go away to college because during the school year, his mother made him come straight home, and he was not allowed to go outside again. This sounded extreme to me at the time, but it was his mother's way of protecting him from the violence of the streets, and insisting that he stay focused on school. The success stories in failing schools are amazing, but they are few. There are many more young students who cannot take the pressure. In an environment where violence prevails, a student who takes school seriously can be seen as weak. I have seen numerous students transfer in from other schools in the middle of the school year, and I have watched how the other students influence them easily. As new students, they want to fit in, and this desire often overpowers the desire to do well in school.

In January, Carl transferred from a suburban school in Ohio. He had been living with his mother, but he moved to Philly to live with his father for the remainder of the year. He was an "A" student, and I remember being pleasantly surprised on his first day, when he asked me to clarify the homework assignment, showing me his interest in his work. He was in a class with several boys with behavioral problems, who refused to work in class. In addition, out of eighteen students, six were Special Education students, and could not read at grade level. Like most high school students, Carl wanted to make friends and fit in. Most of the other boys in the class were low performing, uninterested in school, and were frequently defiant and disrespectful. Within a short period, Carl was trying hard to make friends with these kids. He started to work less, stopped paying attention, and his grades started to slip. Eventually, I was able to talk to him and get him to refocus, but he would have performed better and excelled more in a class with other students who were equally as motivated. He lost many months of precious learning time. This is a serious problem in failing schools—so many young people lose years of valuable time, time that could be spent preparing for a better life after high school. The public school system is so understaffed, unprepared, and underequipped to serve these needy children effectively that they graduate at seventeen or eighteen years old without a decent education. By that time, for poor inner-city kids, it is too late. Once they have graduated from high school, many young people no longer have access to institutions like schools that could offer them options. Instead, the schools can only offer them a diploma—and because of our ill-equipped school system, it represents very little achievement.

The pull and influence of other students is strong, especially when there is little discipline and few boundaries set at home. In the inner-city failing schools, many of the children come from unstable homes, and they look to their friends for security. If your friends are defiant and unmotivated, then it is easier to go along with them than to be the odd one out. These pressures apply to many high schools, but in the inner city the risks are greater, and the dangers are more real. Some students can easily access guns, and many have friends or relatives who are involved in the business of drugs. Just associating with certain kids can at a minimum totally change an educational career, and at worst, put a student into life and death situations.

Violence is a daily presence in failing schools. Children of poverty, especially in Philadelphia consider violence to be the go-to method of solving problems. Many learn it at home, and those who don't, see it in the neighborhoods, in the halls, in the classroom and walking home from school. If someone says something to anger you, punching or hitting him or her is a common solution. Even students who might not be considered troublemakers have to live with the violence. One of my students last year, a very quiet girl who came regularly to class, approached me in last period of the day. She asked if she could use my phone to call her sister. I soon learned that she was afraid to walk home because some girls had threatened to "jump her," because she had talked to someone's boyfriend. I offered to walk her home, but eventually she walked with a security guard the few blocks to her house. She made it home, but then missed more than two weeks of school because she was afraid to leave her house. This problem had started months before, and was now resurfacing. The threats that she received kept her out of school for a total of two months. Later that week, as I left the building, I had to run behind a cement wall when a car drove by spraying bullets in my direction. There were roughly ten little children running for cover as I ran behind the wall. At least I was on my way to catch a bus to go home; these children lived in the neighborhood and grew up with this kind of fear every day. This close contact with violence can cause anyone stress and anxiety.

It is well known that in poverty-stricken neighborhoods, young people have fewer role models. I have had numerous conversations with parents of failing students. After explaining to the parent that their child was failing, many times, the parent would turn to the child and say, "Just get a 'D' and pass the class." These are the expectations of many parents in failing schools. They cannot help their children to work harder and set goals for themselves, most likely because they are under stress due to poverty or other factors. Oftentimes, the parents barely graduated from high school themselves, so they do not know how to be successful in school. Some children have told me, "My mom said she hated school too, so she says for me just to try to get a 'D.'"

Because parents' expectations are often very low, many kids have little confidence, and put forth minimal effort. Many students think that coming to class is good enough, and that by just showing up, they deserve credit. Too many parents send their children to school, and then are not at all involved in what their children are doing, even when it comes to their quarterly grades. At the schools where I have taught in Philadelphia, parents are supposed to come to school to pick up their child's report card, and then come to talk to the teacher if needed. At the end of the quarter, the school would usually give the parents three days to come up to the school to pick them up. As teachers, we would wait in our rooms. Usually only two to three parents would show up. The rest of the kids would wait until the principal released the report cards four to five days later. At that point, the parents might see the report cards or they may not. If, however, the child is senior, and a parent finds out that he or she might not graduate, then they will come up to the school to make a fuss. Many times, either the parent or students scream at the teacher for giving him a failing grade. By this time, it is several years too late. The child has barely passed the required courses. Maybe the student has to make up one or two classes over the summer, which can be easily accomplished in a few weeks. At that point, the student gets a high school diploma that represents very little learning.

It takes someone with a very strong will to be able to block everything out and focus on work in the chaotic environment of a failing school. Those who have a hard time concentrating, or get easily distracted can get easily thrown off track by student disruptions, fights, and verbal assaults (all common occurrences in failing schools). In this type of climate, students fall behind, get drawn into the drama and disorder, and become sucked into the general apathy. So who is losing out in these classrooms? All of the children are losing out: the good students (the ones who want to learn) have to fight against and try to rise above all the turmoil. The failing students are not getting the services they need and fall further behind, the Special Education students are not being taught by Special Education teachers, and do not get the services they are entitled to, and the kids in the middle do the bare minimum to get "Cs" and "Ds." If the good students were in classes with other kids of similar skill level, they might excel beyond what they achieve in a failing school. They would benefit from being more challenged. These are often the students whose parents pull them out to enroll them in charter schools. The lower-skilled students have no extra services such as tutoring, or one-on-one help to get them up to speed. These students need special attention and services. All students are affected by the challenges of failing schools. A lot of this could be solved by hiring more specialized teachers, and creating separate classes that address different students' specific needs.

Children who have a hard time functioning in this environment do not excel, and they learn very little. After four years, they receive a high school diploma. Teachers are not offered classes on how to address the effects of poverty, or how to teach to students with behavioral problems and learning disabilities, even when these students often make up to 40 percent of the students in our classes. Administrators are not equipped to deal with these issues, and the school district chooses to ignore them.

Every day, the stress from financial and family issues creates problems for these students. It has been documented that the chronic stress that comes from poverty can be especially damaging to adolescents, whose brains are still growing and going through changes.[15] According to Eric Jensen, "exposure to chronic or acute stress is debilitating. The most common adaptive behaviors include increased anxiety (as manifested in generalized anxiety disorders or post-traumatic stress disorder) and an increased sense of detachment and helplessness. In schools where violence is prevalent and considered by many to be an acceptable means of expression (which is most Philadelphia inner-city schools), these feelings of hopelessness and anxiety are often played out in verbal aggression and physical fights. "This giving up process is known as learned helplessness. It is not genetic; it is an adaptive response to life conditions. And sadly, it takes hold as early as the first grade."[16] In the elementary school years, students are giving up, and from that point on, school is viewed as another stressor—students who do not do well face years of discipline in school, and develop a negative attitude about education. It does not represent a place of hope and learning, and therefore, a way to create a better future, instead, for many children; it becomes a place of failure, struggle, and a reminder of one's shortcomings.

These children become immune to getting in trouble. A common response to numerous situations is "I don't fucking care." They don't care if they get in trouble, they don't care if they get bad grades, and they don't care if they get suspended. In schools where students can see a bright future, they will respond to the consequences of bad behavior. In failing schools, there is little incentive to work hard. Many spend most of their school years receiving disciplinary action, but nothing changes. It affects their grades; they barely pass, but most likely will eventually get a high school diploma. In a suburban school, you might hear similar stories about only a handful of unruly students. In failing schools, this story can be applied to hundreds and hundreds of students. Is this because the teachers are incompetent? No, these are children who unfortunately make up a huge percentage of inner city kids and are affected by the poverty around them. These are problems that are particular to failing schools. Imagine being a teacher who has so many discipline problems in his class, that you are writing eight to ten detentions a day. Most teachers get so bogged down, that they start only writing them for four to five students, the worst offenders. These methods are obviously not working if this is the system that is employed year after year. If these children are acting out because of environmental stressors, as long as the environment stays the same, the punitive actions most likely won't make much of a difference.

What can schools do to address the root problems? We cannot go to a child's home and make them do their homework at night. The parents of kids with behavioral problems are often off the hook when it comes to parenting. Most people would agree that it is the parent's responsibility to make sure that their child is following through with school obligations. If teaching a child responsibility isn't being addressed at home, then should it be taught at school? Research has shown that teaching children coping and stress-relieving skills can help decrease the sense of hopelessness and hostility that is so prevalent in these environments. However, most schools do not provide these services, mostly because they are costly, and public school budgets today are continuously being cut, not augmented. Schools need more counselors and mental health professionals, young adults who can act as a big brother/big sister/parent who will care about and help monitor a child's health, schoolwork, and guide the students to make better decisions. These services need to be offered in elementary schools, so that young people can be supported throughout their school years. If we don't address these problems when the children are young, it is often too late to make changes when the child is fifteen or sixteen. At this age, many children have experienced poor nutrition, poor study habits, the inability to suppress anger, depression, and other mental health issues for years, and it is much more difficult to make changes without professional help. It is for this reason that is so hard to go into a failing high school and expect to turn around a school in a year or two. Many educational reformists today expect that if we just get some excellent teachers into the schools, we should be able to turn everyone around. This way of thinking excludes and ignores the underlying problems that stem from poverty.

Take for example, Marquese, who lives with his mother and his sister in an apartment in North Philadelphia. He went to neighborhood elementary school and middle school close to home, and now attends Vaux. His mother does not work; she has a disability and is on public assistance. His younger sister is in the seventh grade. Marquese barely passes his classes. He gets into trouble frequently, because he has a difficult time staying in his seat. He frequently gets up to walk around, and often will just walk out of the room without permission. He has not been evaluated as a Special Education student, but he could definitely benefit from more individualized attention. He cannot sit still long enough to do his work. He is easily distracted, and prefers to sit and chat with his friends until he gets bored, when he might get up and leave to wander the halls. The hall police see him, and bring him back to class. I called home many times, and mailed home letters to let his mother know what was happening in my class. She never responded to the calls or the letters. Even if his mother did ask to have him tested, and he was found to need Special Education services, he would probably not receive them due to the district's lack of resources.

Keisha was a Special Education student at the second Promise Academy where I taught. She read at the third grade level, and she was in the eleventh grade. She was very low functioning, which means that on her own, she had an extremely difficult time doing schoolwork. Like most of the girls, she would walk into class with nothing more than a purse. She did not bring a writing utensil, so the one or two times that she did any work, she demanded a pen. She had an extremely defiant personality, and rarely came to class, possibly showing up six to eight times a month. Because she was a SPED student, she knew that by law she could not be failed, which meant that she could come to class two times a week, do very little work, and she was guaranteed to pass the class. Most SPED students know this, so they do just that. Instead of coming to class, they cut, wander the halls, hide out in another part of the building, or just walk out of the building in the middle of the day and don't come back. Four years later, they graduate with a diploma. Our school system allows this, largely because there is no funding to get more SPED teachers, and because there are no support services in place to help them.

According a report published by the Alliance for Excellent Education in 2010, "Although the lowest-performing high schools are spread throughout the country and vary greatly in size and locale, their unifying characteristic is the prevalence of poor and minority students attending them. These schools typically serve a larger number of students living in poverty than the average high school. Minority students make up three quarters of the total enrollment of low performing high schools; almost twice the rate for students of color in all high schools nationwide."[17]

A large percentage of failing schools in Philadelphia are located in disadvantaged urban areas. The families from these neighborhoods often have economic problems that cause stress on the children, and affect their ability to learn. Persistent hardships from poverty have a detrimental effect on the poor child's entire school career. Many often grow up in crowded households, where the parent is overwhelmed with financial issues, and school is not a priority. Research has shown correlations between low income and psychiatric disorders, social and academic functioning, and chronic physical health problems. Most children living in poverty come to school far less prepared than students of higher socio-economic status, who come to school with larger vocabularies, and generally experience more support, encouragement, and attention at home.

In failing urban schools, there are an alarmingly high number of mentally retarded students. They come from poor families, who are not equipped to provide them with the needed services. According to the Arc Greater Twin Cities (Minnesota), poverty is one of the major causes of mental retardation in our country.

> Poverty, whether in a rural or urban setting brings together all the necessary ingredients for mental retardation. Chances are the child born in poverty will encounter more obstacles to his intellectual development in the first years of his life than a middle class youngster will face during his entire life. Even before birth, the basis for retardation may be established for the baby if his mother does not receive proper prenatal care. The President's Committee on Mental Retardation reports that 75 percent of these people could be self-supporting if given the right kind of training early enough.
>
> Some of the contributing factors to mental retardation include the following:
>
> 1. Prenatal problems, such as using alcohol, drugs, or smoking during pregnancy. Other risks include malnutrition, certain environmental contaminants, and illnesses of the mother during pregnancy.
> 2. Childhood diseases and accidents, such as a blow to the head or near drowning. Lead, mercury, and other environmental toxins can cause irreparable damage to the brain and nervous system.

Socioeconomic status: Children in poor families may become mentally retarded because of malnutrition, disease-producing conditions, inadequate medical care, and environmental health hazards. In addition, children in disadvantaged areas may be deprived of many common cultural and day-to-day experiences provided to other youngsters. Research suggests that such under-stimulation can result in irreversible damage and can serve as a cause of mental retardation.[18]

Robert was a senior at Vaux High School while I taught there. On his IEP (Individualized Educational Plan), it stated that he was Mildly Mentally Retarded (MMR). Robert's reading level was below the first grade. He lived just a few blocks from school, and his attendance was spotty at best. I helped in one of the classes that he was enrolled in—Spanish Level Two. (Some teachers questioned why a child who is MMR would be placed in such a difficult class.) This is typical in public high schools. Without the funds and resources, these students are continuously placed into classes that are way above their level. This sets them up for failure. Because of the level of difficulty, they ended up either cutting class every day or coming to class, doing nothing and wasting precious time. Robert rarely showed up to Spanish class because he could barely read English. His teachers called home, and discussed his issues with his Special Education caseworker. The bottom line though, was that the school had no special services to offer a student like Robert. If you asked any of his teachers, they would tell you that he rarely came. He was embarrassed and uncomfortable in class because he understood very little of what was being taught.

You could see Robert at school though-he wandered the halls, snuck into the gym to play basketball with the gym class, or sat on the steps in the stairwell. Always wearing his hair in braids, he was very friendly and respectful. On my way to the bus after school, I would see him riding his bike around the neighborhood, and several times I saw him riding his bike near my home, several miles from school. One day, I was in the office of the director of the Special Ed department. We were talking about the large number of SPED kids who were underserved and forgotten, passed on to the next grade, then out of the school in June of their senior year—totally unprepared to do anything with their lives. Robert's name came up— she used him as an example and said, "We totally dropped the ball with Robert. He should have been enrolled years ago in a life skills program, so that at least he could get a job, and have a productive life." This never happened. She was telling me this a few months before the end of his senior year.

What happened in Robert's educational trajectory? He went to a neighborhood elementary school and a neighborhood middle school. His IEP described a few goals towards which he was supposed to work. However, his skill set was so limited, and there were not enough teachers to give him individualized attention, that the goals were most likely not met. Because of the district mandated inclusion model, Robert took most all of his classes with general education students. Robert received his high school diploma in June. I still see Robert sometimes riding his bike in my neighborhood. He rides the long distance to see friends in South Philly. What will become of Robert? He will most likely continue to live as he does now. If his family doesn't enroll him in a job-training program, he will at least continue to receive public assistance or a social security check.

Poor children start their lives from a point of deprivation for many reasons. Many of their mothers have poor nutrition, some are dependent on alcohol or drugs, and the unborn child suffers. They are often born to mothers under the age of eighteen, and they do not receive the necessary medical care. Young girls who have babies while in high school often leave their children with a family member, so the mother is not as involved in their upbringing. In poor communities in Philadelphia, it would be difficult to stop 15-year-old girls from having babies. But we could educate them about sexuality and birth control, and teach them about their options. At the inner city high schools where I have taught, I have had many students from ninth to twelfth grade who were pregnant, or already had one or two children. These girls had many roadblocks to deal with along the way. Some girls were able to manage, if they had a supportive family. A large number of them slowly stopped coming to class because they had no one to take care of their child.

I had many conversations with these young mothers, and there were few who planned to go on to college. One of my students, Tyneisha, a sixteen-year-old with an eleven-month-old daughter told me, "Well, it is a girl's job to have children." I saw several girls drop out at sixteen and seventeen. They were already receiving a welfare check, so they saw that as a financial option. I got the sense from many of these young people that living on this fixed income was "good enough," and it was difficult to see anything beyond it. For many of them, there was no incentive to break the negative cycle. In a conversation with one of the teachers who worked at the same inner city school for twenty-three years, I learned that many girls know how to work the welfare system to their advantage. Once they have a baby, they qualify for welfare. This benefits the entire family, so it is usually not discouraged by other family members. As soon as they give birth to another child, they are entitled to more money, so there is a definite incentive to continue the cycle, whether there is a father in the picture or not. For many of these young girls, it is easier to have a baby, which is considered acceptable in poor neighborhoods, than to work hard in school, get an education, and go to college.

At this time, many schools in the inner-city offer programs that help young mothers in high school. According to an article in April 2010, in *The Notebook,* a Philadelphia School District newspaper, "An estimated 10,000 to 12,000 Philadelphia teenagers are mothers. According to Project U-Turn, about 70 percent are not likely to graduate due to demands of raising children, finances, lost academic time, and lack of child care."[19] One student wrote in to the newspaper, *"hi my name is celia and i am 14 and pregnant i have always been a straight a student but my first time i made a mystake and got pregnant and now i dont know were im goin to school next year because iam scared that i will be harrased anyone have any information for me ? you can contact me on facebook. thankyou for your help*

sincerely, celia"[20]

Life in these poor neighborhoods is a study of the vicious cycle. In high school, large numbers of girls give birth at a young age. They either don't finish high school, or they stop after the twelfth grade. They might find a job, but it is difficult because they have to pay for child care. Many go on public assistance. They don't have the tools to make good decisions for their children. The mothers of most of the children in failing high schools most often are very young and did not attend college. A large number of kids live with another family member or friend. Parents do expect their kids to go to school, but there is little expectation to do much else. Today we are teaching the children of these women who had children at fourteen, fifteen, and sixteen years old.

If schools are failing, are we looking at the root causes? Most educational reformers do not mention poverty. They don't propose ways of supporting these children who come to school every day too traumatized to learn. In fact, many people don't believe that it should be up to a public school to provide social services to children. The reality is though that you cannot apply the same solutions to a failing school in a poor neighborhood that are applied to schools in middle-class neighborhoods. If we do not provide support services to these suffering children, nothing will change. The problems are different, so the solutions must be different. What can we do as a public school system to address these hardships and stress in the children's lives to help them become successful? If we are not honestly looking at the root causes, we are not going to come up with solutions that will bring about change.

When you compare urban children born in poverty to children of higher-income households, the contrasts are staggering. Children in poverty-stricken neighborhoods are exposed to stressors every day that children in the suburbs never experience. Most of these neighborhoods (especially in Philadelphia, which has a ghetto in almost every area of the city) are high traffic areas, so the children grow up playing in busy streets. They have fewer parks to play in, many live in run-down housing, and in overcrowded households that allow for very little private or study time. Children in poverty tend to watch more TV, have fewer reading materials at home, and have fewer cognitive-enrichment activities. Many do not have access to computers at home, which hinders their ability to read and research for school. They also have less access to healthy foods, as most of the children often buy their "meals" at the corner stores, which are located on many corners in the neighborhoods, and offer little more than a 7-11. Many of my students would tell me it was rare to sit down to a meal at home, that they often got dinner at the neighborhood Chinese takeout place, or they would buy a hoagie or cheese steak from the corner store. These are young children who live in stressful environments inside and outside of their home.

According to Eric Jensen, in *Teaching with Poverty in Mind*, "Common issues in low-income families include depression, chemical dependence, and hectic work schedules-all factors that interfere with the healthy attachments that foster children's self-esteem, sense of mastery of their environment, and optimistic attitudes. Instead poor children often feel isolated and unloved, feelings that kick off a downward cycle of events, including poor academic performance, behavioral problems, dropping out of school, and drug abuse."[21]

Students come to school under stressful conditions and teachers are affected too. Even though the schools in which I have worked have had great teachers, the conditions in which they work are so difficult, that many quit or transfer out. This only creates more instability and uncertainty in these students' lives. When kids do not have someone to talk to at home, a teacher can often become a valuable source of support. However, so many teachers transfer out of these schools after one year, that students lose that source, and then become hesitant to form relationships with teachers, for fear of being disappointed yet again.

Studies show that children who grow up in poverty often do not grow up in loving, nurturing homes. Poor families often experience financial instability, health problems and other stressors that can negatively affect the chance for a loving, sensitive relationship between child and caregiver. These unstable relationships can later affect a student's ability to develop positive bonds with peers, teachers, and authority figures. The feelings of despair that low-income parents often experience are communicated and passed on to the children. These sentiments of depression and inability to cope are expressed in the classroom, and manifest themselves in negative behavior, refusal to participate, and apathy. We need to provide training to teachers about how poverty affects schoolchildren, how to help them to be successful. We also need to develop school-based programs where professionals can offer ongoing counseling to students of need.

Research shows that social risk factors such as unemployment, poverty, drug abuse, and high population density are all associated with high rates of violence. The high population density is often a result of young teenage girls having children in high school, and many family members living together in one household. As a teacher, the never-ending cycle is apparent every day. Alarming numbers of my young female students are either pregnant or already have one or two children. They are struggling in school, at risk of dropping out or barely graduating. They are fifteen, sixteen, and seventeen years old. From a middle class perspective, it is difficult to understand the choices these young girls make.

According to Elijah Anderson, author of *Code of the Street*, poor, black teenagers growing up in the ghettos of Philadelphia see pregnancy and motherhood as something positive, as it might create the family that the young girl does not have and bring attention from the baby's father. "The girls have a dream of being carried off by a Prince Charming who will love them, provide for them, and give them a family ... She wants desperately to believe that if she becomes pregnant, he will at least be more obligated to her than other girls he has been 'messing with' …The boys desire either sex without commitment or babies without the responsibility for them."[22] Unfortunately, many young teenage boys are not mature enough, nor do they have the tools to help the young mothers, and the responsibility goes to the mother and grandmothers. Many do not see opportunities for the future, so the young girls do not perceive pregnancy as something that would get in the way of creating a successful life for themselves.

When teachers try to reach out to many of the parents in inner-city schools, there is often very little support to be found. These young girls, many of whom are barely passing school as it is, are getting pregnant today, and five years from now, their children will be entering the public school system. The young mothers are often still on public assistance, either barely graduated or dropped out of high school, and not prepared to be involved, proactive parents. This cycle will continue, year after year unless we put programs in place in the communities and schools to show these young girls that they have options.

In 2011, 25 percent of the population lived below the poverty line in Philadelphia.[23] In addition, the city has a historically high violence rate. According to the Philadelphia Research Initiative, Philadelphia is more violent than all but seven of the nation's fifty largest cities, trailing only Detroit, Memphis, Oakland, Baltimore, Cleveland, Kansas City, and Washington, DC. At the time the 2011 report came out, the unemployment rate was at 11.5 percent. In the same year, 42 percent of the population was African American, 12 percent Hispanic, and 37 percent was non-Hispanic. In the last few years, when "flash mobs" were becoming popular all over the country, they had a different meaning in Philly. In New York City, it meant people convened in Times Square to dance together. In Philly, a flash mob meant that after receiving a text message, groups of teenagers would meet downtown and start randomly beating up people on the street. One particular night during the summer of 2011, about twenty to thirty youths met in the downtown area after dark, and then punched, beat, and robbed bystanders. Some shop owners locked their doors to keep customers inside for protection. Several people were hospitalized, and the police arrested four youth, including one eleven-year-old boy.

Many children in Philadelphia grow up with violence as a part of their daily lives. Repeated exposure to violence has a negative impact on children and adolescents. A report on children's exposure to violence by the Child's Trend Data Bank, states that "an experience of violence can lead to lasting physical, mental, and emotional harm, whether the child is a direct victim or a witness. Children who are exposed to violence are more likely to suffer from attachment problems, regressive behavior, anxiety, and depression, and to have aggression and conduct problems. Other health-related problems, as well as academic and cognitive problems include delinquency, and involvement in the child welfare and juvenile justice systems."[24]

In Philadelphia, my students talk about violence all day long. When faced with a situation that angers them, a common reaction is, "I'm gonna punch him in his face! Or I'm gonna fuck him up!" They have not learned other coping strategies from home or outside the school. Teachers at our school last year frequently discussed the need for classes to teach students how to communicate in ways that are more constructive. In a financially stable neighborhood, these skills are usually learned at home, and when high school age children enter school, it is expected that they know how to conduct themselves appropriately. In Philadelphia, many children see and hear aggressive behavior at home and in the neighborhoods on a daily basis, and it spills over into the classrooms. Often they have not learned how to communicate effectively, and turn to violence first as a way to express a wide variety of emotions: fear, anger, and frustration.

Lemar was a senior when I taught him at Vaux High School. He was very respectful to me and always came into class on time fully dressed in his uniform, including the navy blue blazer, which most kids refused to wear. He was in the Special Education program, but he had the ability to stay focused and on task. He would take good notes, pay attention, and turn in his work on time. One day, when I asked Lemar why he seemed so tired, he told me that the night before the police had burst into the house at two in the morning, ransacking the place where he lived with his mother and sister. They were looking for his brother, who was wanted on drug charges, but were unable to locate him. He described the event as if it was just another day, except for the interruption to his sleep, which made him drowsy that afternoon. Several weeks later, Jamal, a classmate of his, started to tease him, and Lemar responded with his own comments. The teasing turned quickly into taunting, and within minutes, the boy had walked over and started to threaten Lemar physically. Lamar, who was at least a foot shorter than Jamal, pushed him against the wall, reached up, and grabbed the boy by the throat, and in a matter of seconds was squeezing his neck so hard that I could see that Jamal was unable to breathe. I screamed for him to stop, and then ran to the phone to call for help. Luckily, a security guard came within a few minutes, broke it up and they were hauled off to the principal's office. To see the panic in Jamal's eyes as his air supply was being cut off was extremely frightening for me and upset me for the rest of the day. The impact of this experience stayed with me, and yet I was able to leave school and go home to a peaceful house, something that many of these kids do not have the luxury to do.

According to studies, "One mechanism through which early, chronic exposure to violence affects children is by disrupting the developing brain. Specific brain structures ... are adversely affected by stress. Executive functions (such as planning, memory, focusing attention, impulse control, and using new information to make decisions) can become impaired. Moreover, children who have had chronic exposure to real or perceived threats may become conditioned to react with fear and anxiety to a broad range of circumstances."[25]

Young people who are continuously exposed to violence become unable to differentiate between genuine threats and objectively safe situations. This hurts their ability to communicate with others and can lead to serious anxiety disorders. The children in Philadelphia's inner city grow up in neighborhoods where violence is a way of life, and they bring these problem-solving methods to school. When a teacher has large classrooms of 28-33 children, it is extremely difficult to reach those who are struggling with emotional problems. Furthermore, if a teacher identifies that a student is having emotional problems, often the only people usually available are the school nurse or the guidance counselor, who is usually trained to help students with their school schedules, not emotional issues.

Out of the five high schools where I have taught, only one has had a Special Education teacher who specialized in emotional problems. One Special Education teacher cannot possibly address all of the issues in a failing inner city school. It is clear that many students are far behind not only in academics, but also in social development. All of the negative factors, such as violence in their communities and lack of support at home, make it extremely difficult for them to progress developmentally. Many are anywhere from four to five years behind their age group in maturity level, and lack coping and communication skills.

According to the American Psychological Association, "Poorer children and teens are also at greater risk for several negative outcomes such as poor academic achievement, school dropout, abuse and neglect, behavioral and socioemotional problems, physical health problems, and developmental delays. Children who are exposed to violent behavior are more likely to act violently towards others."[26] When they came to class, these students refuse to work, and pick fights with other students.

The violence is not limited to high schools either. In the *Philadelphia Inquirer's* report on violence in the schools, the article discussed how violence is prevalent in the elementary schools as well.

Tabitha Allen blames herself for her ten-year-old son's behavior. Growing up and living in a drug-infested, hooker-inhabited neighborhood, the thirty-three-year-old mother of five is angry about life. "My anger reflects off my children," Allen explained one morning in the North Philadelphia row house she inherited from her grandmother. Her son—a thin, almost gaunt boy with long eyelashes—punched a teacher last June at Kenderton Elementary School, a K-8 in Tioga. He knocked the glasses off her face and blackened an eye with a blow that packed unexpected power. Another incident occurred in South Philly. At Southwark Elementary, a K-8 school in South Philadephia, in October 2010, a ten-year-old boy "body-slammed" his teacher with such force that she suffered a concussion as she fell to the ground. In April 2008, in a third grade classroom at Taylor Elementary, a K-5 school in Hunting Park, one child held a knife against a classmate's throat and threatened to cut his head off if he snitched.[27]

Come into one of my classrooms and look around, and you will see a lot of different coping mechanisms. Some students deal with the pain by withdrawing. They are quiet and unresponsive. Many more deal with it by acting out, picking fights with teachers and other students. But almost all of them are coping alone, with little to no help. In Philadelphia, most administrators and district representatives believe that teachers should figure it out by themselves. Many students are hurting so much inside, that they only way they know how to cope is to react with aggressive behavior. Attacks like the one that Tasheda Harris experienced are common. Our superintendent at the time, Arlene Ackerman, said of the issue, "When young people rush into a classroom, when they roam the halls, that's an adult problem—of the educators in that school." But when you are one female teacher in the classroom, and a group of students, (many of whom are a foot taller and weigh up to a hundred pounds more than the teacher) storms in, it is a challenge to control them. When students act aggressively and are hell-bent on hurting another student, it is difficult to reason with them. Usually, the only thing you can do is get on the phone and call the security guard. At the high school where I taught in 2012, we had a police officer on every floor during classes. On my floor, the officer had formerly been a prison guard. He was big, tough, and effective. When kids would start fighting in the classroom, he was there to take them away. In January, however, there were rumors of budget cuts to the security employees, and one day we came to school and he was gone. In the next few days, he had been replaced with older, senior guards who were close to retirement. They were slower to react, and not as effective, but money was scarce.

In the *Inquirer* article about violence in Philly schools, it was reported that "in the district's thirty-two neighborhood high schools… the violence rate increased 17 percent over five years—to 51.1 percent reported incidents of violence per 1,000 students in 2009–10."[28] Nearly three-quarters of the schools reporting violent incidents had at least one teacher who had been assaulted. The article also stated that these numbers might not even be accurate, because many principals do not report all of the incidents (as was the case at Vaux). Many of these Philadelphia schools are in neighborhoods threatened by poverty, crime, hunger, drugs and parental neglect, and many of the schools are failing or turn-around schools.

It is often difficult to get principals to support you when it comes to violence in the classroom. Most principals and vice-principals in failing schools are dealing with violent behavior all day long. Their offices are often like revolving doors, with disruptive and violent students coming in and out for punishment. They are overwhelmed, just as teachers are. Because they have so much to deal with, they are frequently not receptive to teachers asking for help. "You knew what you were getting into. Handle your class. Maybe you should find another school if you can't handle these kids," are all comments I have heard from principals of my schools. When the Philadelphia Inquirer asked school district officials about how teachers and staff should deal with violence in the classrooms, district spokesperson Shana Kemp said: "Individuals who are assaulted, parents, students, teachers, and staff must file individual criminal charges. Not the school." Unfortunately, most principals do not agree, and get angry when a teacher calls to press charges. Two African American female teachers at my school were physically threatened last year. They both called 911 from the classroom. Police officers from the nearest precinct came up to take the report, and they pressed assault charges against them. A month later, when three different students threatened me in one morning, I contacted the police. When the principal found out, I was reprimanded. "Maybe you should find another school if you can't handle it," she said to me. When the police came up to the school to take the report, the female officer implied that I was lying about the incident, and refused to do anything about it. I had no choice but to go back to my room and teach the next class. Knowing the climate of the school, and the history of retaliation from the principal, I let it drop. Even though I was angry that the principal did not care about the safety of her teachers, I did not want to pursue the issue further. My job was at stake. If I made waves in any way, the principal could come into my classroom and write up an unfavorable evaluation, as she had already done with many other teachers. It was too close to the end of the year, and I needed a job for the next fall. I couldn't risk it.

According to the *Philadelphia Inquirer*, in the year 2010, 690 teachers were assaulted; in the last five years, 4,000 were assaulted."[29] One assault happened at Lincoln High School:

Veteran Philadelphia school teacher Lou Austin endured forty minutes of terror as the fifteen-year-old ninth grader jabbed his index finger into Austin's temple and threatened to kill him while swinging a pair of scissors menacingly. Austin didn't even know the youth, who ransacked his classroom—flipping desks and attempting to set fire to books—at Lincoln High School in Mayfair on Valentine's Day. He'd merely asked him to step away from his classroom door and go to his own class when the youth exploded. "All I could do was to stand there with my hands behind my back, accept the abuse, and hope this did not infuriate him even more," said Austin, a Philadelphia teacher for fifteen years who graduated from Lincoln in 1984."[30]

Teachers in inner city failing schools today have so many more issues to deal with than just academics.

The fact that many teachers in Philadelphia can read about this account without batting an eyelash is indicative of how widespread the problem is, and how numb we have become to the violence. As inner-city public school teachers, nothing surprises us anymore, because we see it every day, all day long. The violence is not just directed at other students. Teachers are fair game, and the administration will often not back teachers up. Administrators will frequently turn the story around and try to hold the teacher responsible when a student threatens an educator. It would take much more than "great teachers" to solve these problems. Unless we either train teachers in how to deal with violence and poverty, or invest money into services to help these children, nothing will change. The problem is too big. It is time to be realistic and address the true roadblocks to achievement. We need to face the problems of violence that comes from growing up in poor neighborhoods, and set up mentor and counseling programs that can provide these kids with the help they need.

Interventions for students with learning disabilities, anger problems, anxiety, aggression, and depression cost money. As discussed in chapter six, Geoffrey Canada has built a network of support services for his students in Harlem at the Harlem Children's Zone (HCZ). HCZ reported a total revenue of $69 million dollars in 2010 (HCZ has a total of three schools). They offer health care services, legal guidance, financial advice, debt relief counseling, domestic crisis resolution, and parenting classes for young mothers, among other services. In the same year, I was at Vaux High School. This was the first year of the turnaround program, and the first year the school was a "Promise Academy." We had an enrollment of 425 students, with a poverty rate of 94.2 percent. According to the Philadelphia School District budget report, our school budget for that year was $3,928,736. This was the first year of the Promise Academy model, and the district had received federal stimulus money to help fund these turn-around schools. At the end of the 2010/2011 school year, the district announced the budget cuts. Many cuts were made to the operating budget and school safety in the last two years. Even though violence is a huge problem in Philadelphia schools, school safety and nursing services are often one of the first areas to be cut.

Vaux High School Budget 2010-2013[31]

	2010/2011	2011/2012	2012/2013
Enrollment	425	403	360
Poverty rate	94.2%	94.8%	94.1%
Teachers	1,464,750	1,379,700	1,319,700
Operating budget	1,465, 387	871,133	692,220
Music program	9,460	9,460	0
Nursing services	102,200	41,200	43,680
School safety	94,600	41,000	40,000
Total budget	2,463,986	3,099,299	2,736,360
Subtotal: Operating funded allotments	3,928,736	3,099,299	2,736,390
Change from previous year	--	-21.1%	-11.7%
Subtotal: Excluding enrollment teachers	2,463,986	1,719,599	1,416,890
Change from previous year		-30.2%	-17.6%

As evidenced in the table above, over the last few years money has become scarcer, and services have been dropped from the Vaux High School budget. What started out in the beginning of the 2010/2011 school year as "the new Promise Academies," which the principal referred to several times throughout the year as "the Promise Academy movement," was soon down to such a compromised budget, that it no longer resembled anything different from before. Instead, it looked suspiciously like the school of five years ago, with a limited budget to address students' needs. In fact, even when the school opened as a Promise Academy, the district never thought to provide special services for emotionally disturbed or poor students. If you compare the budget of Harlem Children's Zone with the budget of Vaux High School, you can see that there is a huge difference in available money to spend on student programs. Even though corporate reformers continue to say that it's not about the money, they use the Harlem Children's Zone as an example of a school that works—with three schools and $69 million dollar budget, they have roughly seven times the budget of Vaux High School to spend on services for each school. If we want students to succeed in public schools, funding is needed to offer services to support them. What is the alternative? A continuous cycle of uneducated young people released into the workforce, underprepared and under skilled to compete in today's job market.

The loudest and most influential voices in the reform movement are wealthy special interest groups who are far removed from the problems of real classrooms. Rarely do these reformists ask those people most affected by school issues, like parents, students, and teachers about what they believe are needed in our schools. Their goals, if motivated by monetary gain, focus on how to profit from change, not how to ensure that the children will benefit from it. Let's use the Harlem Children's Zone as a model for our public schools. Why take that money away from the poor who cannot access charters and private schools? Instead, focus on the children who could potentially perform at much higher levels if given the proper tools. It will take funding and leadership. If we only fund charters and online schools for the fortunate few who escape failing schools, we will allow the rest of the children to fail. Even though we know that family income is the single most reliable factor in student test scores, policy makers and corporate reformers choose to ignore this, and have no proposals that address the effects of poverty and violence on our nation's inner-city children. What will happen to our neighborhood schools in crime-infested areas of our large cities, if more charter schools are created? What will happen to the already precarious situation of violence, crime, and poverty?

Research over the last twenty years has shown that poverty, as defined as the absence of sufficient income to cover basic expenses and inequality, discrimination and institutional racism account for increased violence in minority groups. In poor African American neighborhoods, "the over-representation of variables such as segregation, family disruption, joblessness, social isolation, and sparse social networks, in addition to limited financial resources"[32] all contribute to the prevalence of violence. In their description of the contributors to the failures of black students, the anthropologists and authors Signithia Fordham and John Ogbu, include "the extent to which some minorities respond to social inequity by developing what has been labeled as oppositional social identity and an oppositional cultural reference."[33]

Minority students growing up in poor underserved neighborhoods see hopelessness every day and often react with anger and violence. Further research has shown that many black teenagers, when faced with the difficulties of navigating the status mobility system of American culture (school, college, the job market), to attain basic needs such as food, shelter and medical care, many turn to negative means, such as violence and crime. "Their capacity to perpetuate violence is the great equalizer in a world characterized by great inequalities."[34]

Children who grow up in poverty, and attend schools in underserved neighborhoods rarely seek psychological help. In cases where adolescents witness violence, or are victims of violence, including rape, stabbings, and shootings, very few report the incidents or seek medical attention. This can have huge implications in later years, because of the devastating psychological effects. In the cases of young children, they come to school with the burden of these experiences.

In inner-city schools, teachers see the effects of poverty every day. Contrary to the belief of many wealthy reformers, poverty *does* get in the way of learning. To deny this is social injustice. Of course there are poor children who are capable of doing well in school. But on the other hand, many are not, because they are too traumatized by family tragedy, poverty and violence. Not only do they need help with their math and reading, they need help dealing with the stresses of growing up in poor, violent neighborhoods.

If schools could establish counseling centers in the schools that would be safe and welcoming havens for these kids who are suffering, it would be a positive step in helping to alleviate the pressures that impede their learning. So many of these children do not have an adult that they trust and can talk to. Without the attention and help from a caring adult, more children slip through the system. Wealthy reformers tell the public that the problems aren't about money, and that public schools have plenty of money to work with. However, it takes money to pay the salaries of support people, psychologists, counselors, mentors, and nurses—money that is not available. Partnerships with college students could be effective, especially with universities who have students interested in psychology, education, law, social work or other areas where college students could utilize their research and experience to positively influence and guide them.

In Philadelphia, just as in other big cities, there are a number of large universities that are great resources for mentors. The principals of city public schools should take advantage of these programs and create partnerships with universities. College students can be good role models for at-risk youth. It could mean the difference between a child giving up on school, and finding a way to refocus and work towards an education and a better future. The bottom line is teachers need a support system to supplement what they do in the classroom, so that they can focus on academics.

Chapter Three

NO LONGER A
SPECIAL EDUCATION

Lawrence came into class yelling out at the top of his voice, "What's up motherfuckers?" "Lawrence, please take your seat." Ignoring me, he kept on walking. He sat down next to a girl in the back of class. I walked over to redirect him. He got up and walked the other way, stopping to sit down again next to another student. "Lawrence, I need you to sit down in your seat. Let's go." After finally sitting at his desk, but still talking loudly, I gave him his folder, and I explained his assignment. He started working, and I proceeded to address the rest of the class.

"Cockadoodle-doo!" I turned to see Lawrence, who with his head thrown back, was crowing like a rooster. He worked for five minutes, then got up and walked around the room.

Special Education is defined as the education of students with special needs, such as: students with learning disabilities, communication issues, emotional, developmental, or behavioral disorders. Problems are often identified in elementary school, and if a teacher or parent feels that a student might need special services, they can request an evaluation. If the evaluation shows that the student needs additional attention, then a Special Education teacher will write up the IEP (Individualized Educational Plan), which outlines the student's needs and learning goals. The IEP is a legal document, and a parent has the right to make sure that it is followed by all of the child's teachers. It states the student's level of performance in reading and math, the specific goals the student has for the year, and the accommodations that must be made to help him or her. The IEP can be amended over the years, if a teacher or parent sees a need to change the learning goals or expectations.

Lawrence's IEP stated that he read at a sixth grade level. The rest of the information on the IEP described his goals for English and math class. If you teach another subject, such as science, social studies, or a world language, the only relevant information on the document is the reading level. The student may have serious learning problems or mild ADHD, but this information is not given to the teacher. There is no information about psychological or behavior problems. As teachers, we must figure that out for ourselves, by asking questions and talking to the Special Education teachers. On this particular day, I must do the best I can with the little bit of information that I have about this student.

A few months into the year, I spoke with the head of the Special Education Department (SPED). I shared with her that I was concerned about Lawrence's ability to perform in my class. He seemed to struggle with severe learning as well as behavior issues, which made it very difficult for him to make progress. I also sensed that there was something else going on with him, perhaps a mental problem, which the IEP did not address. Without wanting to ask this question directly, I said, "What is going on with Lawrence exactly?" Her reply was that he was having "problems at home." I was with him every day in my class, and I knew that something more serious was going on, and did not understand why she would want to keep this information from a teacher who was expected to help him in the classroom. How could I effectively teach him without knowing what his learning issues or other issues were? When I mentioned that his IEP stated that his reading level was at the sixth grade, she responded, "Oh, that information isn't accurate, he actually reads at a much lower level." So, the *only* information that I was given about him was incorrect. I found out later in the year (six months later) that he was pre-schizophrenic. For six months, he had been in general education classes; making little progress because he refused to work more than ten minutes at a time, disrupting the class every day, taking time and attention away from the other students. The learning environment was not benefitting anyone. Lawrence lost precious time, and the rest of the class did as well. Legally, he was entitled to special services, but he was receiving very few. Unfortunately, his mother was in no condition to request more. She had her own serious health issues.

The Special Education teacher made a few suggestions on how to modify his work, but I did not receive any concrete information that would help me to teach him. Every day was a struggle with Lawrence. He was put on a "daily report," which is a document that the student takes to each class, and gives to the teacher at the beginning of the hour to be filled out. There are several boxes that the teacher must check off regarding the student's behavior and work performance in class. This served as a message to the student that I was reporting to his caseworker what was going on in class. It usually brought some positive short-term results; at best, they lasted four days until the student either stopped bringing the report in, or just got tired of having to behave.

I found out later in the year that Lawrence lived with his grandparents in an unstable home. His mother was a drug addict, was diagnosed with schizophrenia, and the school was trying to place him in a hospital. Midway through the year, I was told by another teacher that he had become delusional and was describing situations and places that did not exist. He continued to come to my class, continued to disrupt, and did no work. He might work for a total of eight minutes, get bored, and start walking around the room, or yelling out to other people across the room. When I described this to his case manager, he came to class the next day with a new "daily report."

All the teachers who I spoke with had the same problems that I was having. The head of the Special Education department hinted that it was only happening in my class, but I read the other teachers' comments on the daily report every day:

"Lawrence ran around the room today."

"Lawrence refused to work."

"Lawrence walked out of class."

I added, "Lawrence did cartwheels across the room today."

His behavior was extremely disruptive to the rest of the General Education students in the class. They would often yell at him to be quiet. I had to stop teaching several times during the hour to redirect him, discipline him, physically move him back to his seat, or call security to have him removed. Ultimately, he was placed for a month in an in-treatment facility. The administration had been trying for months to make this happen, but it did not occur until May, one month before the end of school. His placement was delayed because his mother could not get it together to take him to the doctor.

Every time a teacher has to deal with extremely disruptive students, the flow of the class is interrupted and the other students have to wait until the problem is resolved. I was told there was no money to hire someone to help him in my class. We had a team of eight Special Education teachers in our building, but they were busy in other classes. This is the educational experience for many SPED students in the Inclusion Model. They go to their classes, do a minimum of work, and receive a passing grade. Because it is extremely difficult to fail a Special Education student, they can do 1 percent of the assigned work, and they will move to the next grade. They graduate from high school with very little skills and the idea that everything will be "modified" for them in life. Many of these students are capable of much more. Even though some SPED students misbehave in class, there are others who are very capable of progressing at a higher level. Unfortunately, they were only tested once in elementary school, and have carried the Special Education label into high school. They are so accustomed to operating under extremely low expectations, that they become complacent and lazy. The message is very clear to them: "Nothing is expected of you, getting a "D" is the goal, you will pass anyway, so why bother trying?" These are the students who are graduating from our high schools.

One Special Education teacher told me last year, "The problem is that the school district doesn't have enough money to hire psychologists to test kids in middle school and high school. They get tested once in elementary school, then for the rest of their school career, decisions (such as the classes they take, how they will be evaluated, services that they are eligible to receive) are based on that evaluation." Years could go by, and they are not re-tested. From the time of the first evaluation to the time a student graduates from high school, things could change. A student could develop new and different learning problems, or out-grow old ones, and no longer need services. If a child is not retested, he could be stuck in a learning environment that no longer addresses his needs.

At Vaux High School, 30 percent or more of the total population of students were in the Special Education program. This is extremely high (a more common percentage of Special Education students in a public high school would be closer to 10 percent). At Vaux, this meant that in a class of thirty students, ten of them were way behind the rest of the class, read at an elementary school level, or had behavioral problems. There tends to be a lot of movement of students between schools in urban areas, as students move, are transferred or kicked out of other schools, get out of disciplinary schools, or jail. At the beginning of the year, in my third period class, there were sixteen students. Nine were in the Special Education program. The class changed over the year, because some students left to go to other schools, and new students came in. At the end of the year, I had twenty students in that same class. Out of twenty students, ten were Special Education students. The transient nature of urban school populations is very common. Sometimes I would receive two new students in one month. Frequently, they were very far behind. When a student arrives four months into the year, he has a lot of work to do to catch up. In a math or foreign language class, where a great deal of scaffolding of information is essential in the structuring of the curriculum, long lapses in attendance make it extremely hard to be successful. Students who miss weeks or even months of school are at an obvious disadvantage. They come into a class lacking in skills as well as motivation.

In the past, Special Education students were separated from the general population of students. They were in small classes with a Special Education teacher and other students who had similar learning issues. In a smaller class, the teacher can work one-on-one with a child, design lessons to meet their needs, and provide a supportive learning environment. Recently, educators have proposed that when SPED students are separated from the general population, they feel stigmatized. This is never easy for the SPED students. It has been my experience that even in the general education classes, the other students will make fun of them, calling them "dumb," because they quickly see that the SPED students are working on lower level assignments.

The IDEA (The Individuals with Disabilities Education Act) proposes the goal of Least Restrictive Environment (LRE) for SPED students, stating, "*to the maximum extent appropriate, children with disabilities, including children in public or private institutions, or other care facilities, are educated with children who are nondisabled.*"[35] In this Inclusion model, students take all or most of their classes in the General Education classes. Teachers are expected to use teaching methods that address many different learning styles, to differentiate the instruction and to "modify" the lesson to meet the SPED students' needs. This could mean a variety of things, such as giving SPED students lower-level class work or giving them shorter assignments than the general education kids. The concept of inclusion is controversial. Proponents believe that "good" teachers should be able to teach to many different levels in one classroom. Those in opposition feel that trying to teach students of extremely different learning levels in one class is unrealistic and discriminatory. Most of the Special Education teachers at Vaux agreed that the inclusion model does not work for all students and that if it wasn't working for someone, he should be removed from the class and put into a more conducive learning environment. However, at Vaux, it was not up for discussion. When I mentioned to the head of the department that a SPED teacher from another school told me it was probably illegal to have such high numbers of SPED students in one class, she responded, "Not here at the Promise Academy. Our superintendent wants the Inclusion model." Whether it was working or not, that's the way it had to stay, and students lost months and months of precious learning time because of it.

I have had multiple conversations with General as well as Special Education teachers who agree that the inclusion model only works for a very small percentage of students. The rest of them lose time in classes that are way above their ability level, so they are given activities to work on that keep them at their low level. Teachers are not trained in how to teach to eleventh graders who read at a third grade level. These students need specific practice in reading and writing skills before they can tackle other subjects. Public Schools ignore this, and place the students in classes that move too fast, are designed for students who are proficient readers at their grade level, and use vocabulary that is way above their level of understanding. With no one to give them special guidance, they do the bare minimum of work, and most of the time understand very little of the material being taught. Imagine this scenario: Jonathon is a sophomore. He reads at the first grade level. The school counselor enrolls him in a French class. The teacher is instructed by the Special Education department to create worksheets to allow him to participate at his level. She tries this for several weeks. She makes up special worksheets that just focus on colors and pictures, because he struggles with reading.

After three weeks, the rest of the class is moving onto the grammar of the French language, and it becomes increasingly difficult to come up with lessons that are easy enough and fun to keep him engaged. While he is working on his activity, she is trying to teach the rest of the class, which includes seven other Special Education students, who are also struggling. She asks the principal if a SPED teacher could come to help him during class, but he tells her that is not possible, and just to do the best she can. After a couple of months, Jonathan and a couple of the other SPED students start cutting class. It is too hard, there is no one to sit down and explain the concepts, because there are thirty kids in the class, and numerous behavior problems. By May, Jonathan only comes about once a week. He usually goes to the lunchroom to hang out, or sneaks downstairs and hides in the halls. How many hours of precious learning time were lost? If there were more specialized teachers, Jonathan might have been able to spend time working on his reading skills, instead of running from a class that did not fit his needs, and was way above his skill level.

In reality, teachers are expected to teach multiple classes within one. This can be very difficult if the teacher is not given training or materials. Inevitably, someone loses out. Because I only had one set of textbooks for four classes, I went online and purchased elementary level books in my content area to give to my SPED students. The selections were very limited, and not very helpful, so I ended up creating my own exercises for them. Students would usually be expected to listen to the instructional portion of the class, and then work on their own. I would prepare a different lower level activity for the SPED students to work on. General Education teachers often consult the caseworkers about how to evaluate them for a grade. One of my students was Mildly Mentally Retarded (MMR) and read at a kindergarten level. Because her reading skills were so limited, she usually drew pictures or worked on vocabulary exercises in class. She was unable to grasp any of the more difficult concepts that I taught. However, her mother wanted to expose her to the subject. Her caseworker told me to evaluate her solely on effort.

Some of the SPED students can handle the workload, are motivated and self-disciplined. When given their work to focus on, they sit and complete it. However, they are often way behind the rest of the class, so it is hard to build a cohesive lesson that incorporates all the learners effectively. The teacher is still responsible to teach the General Ed students, who are expected to be at grade level. I would estimate that out of eight SPED students in my classes, two could handle the

Inclusion Model. The rest were so frustrated that they refused to work, skipped class, or acted out to avoid having to perform. A lot of time was wasted. If they had been in a smaller classroom with a SPED specialist, they could have made a lot more growth. More often than not, the student needs more individualized attention to be able to make progress. Working with Special Education students is a specialized field (for this reason, SPED teachers make higher salaries), and to take these services away from students with high needs is unfair to them, as well as to the general education students, who deserve to move at a pace that furthers their progress.

In August 2010, teachers reported to Vaux High School for professional development meetings for one week before the school year started. The majority of us were new teachers to the school; however, not necessarily new to teaching. Although there were a significant number of brand new teachers, and teachers who were in the Teach for America program. We had a great group of very capable teachers, but in an environment where a principal can "write you up" if you show insubordination, challenge the procedures, or ask too many questions; the newer teachers without tenure rarely speak out when there are problems. All the teachers knew that they were facing a huge challenge: the school was failing and we were there to make changes.

We met for eight-hour days the week before school started. We covered the procedures of the school, attended workshops on how to make classes more rigorous, and engaging and how to write good lesson plans. The fact that 30 percent of a school's population is in the Special Education program has a huge impact on all of the teachers. Not only did the principal never provide training on how to work with SPED students in a general education classroom, he never even mentioned that 30 percent of the student population was Special Education. Most of us learned this important fact well into the year. As teachers, we started the year without the proper tools to teach these children. At the beginning of the year, teachers are given their class lists. The Special Education department does not usually give the teachers the IEPs until four weeks into the year. Consequently, we are teaching for a month to students with serious learning and behavioral problems, without knowing anything about them. How could we properly educate these students without this information?

Every spring, the Philadelphia public school students take the standardized tests, or PSSAs. (Starting in 2013, the district has switched to a different test called the Keystone Exams.) These tests are a huge part of how schools are evaluated and rated. It is from these scores that Annual Yearly Progress (AYP) is determined. There is a big push to prepare the eleventh graders for the tests from the beginning of the year to test day, usually after the first of the year. This particular year at Vaux, the students took the test over a course of several days. They were divided into several different classrooms for three to four hours in the morning, with two teacher proctors per room. All eleventh graders take the test, even the SPED students. Schools across the country take statewide tests very seriously, because of the implications that they present. In the five high schools where I have taught, there has been a common atmosphere at test time: the school is quiet and rules must be strictly enforced. In the classroom that I proctored at Vaux, it was sometimes a challenge to maintain the serious atmosphere.

There were five students in the room I proctored. Four were SPED students. One was MMR, and read at first grade level. He was given the same test. After a few minutes, he put his head down, because he did not understand the reading. Teachers are not allowed to help, only to say, "Do the best you can." He didn't even bother to ask.

Takierrah and Courtney were working on their tests, until Courtney looked up and caught Takierrah looking at her.

"Stop looking at me!"

"You're ugly, I will fuck you up."

"I can't stand your black ass."

"You're black too!"

"No, I'm light-skinned."

"You're still ugly."

"I'm cuter than you."

"Get outta my face."

"I'm not in your face, because if I was, I would fuck you up."

They did manage to settle down without a physical confrontation, but this scene made a huge impression on me. These tests would be used to evaluate the progress of our school. They were obviously way above the level of comprehension level of the Special Education students, yet the students were not given any accommodations at all. When I asked an administrator about this, she just shrugged, "That's just the way it is."

A large number of the families at Vaux receive public assistance. In addition, those families whose children are in the SPED program receive SSI checks each month of up to $600.00. This money is supposed to be used for services that would help the students in school, such as tutoring. There is no way to determine how a parent is spending the funds. For a single parent on welfare, there is little incentive to get your child off the SPED program if you are receiving SSI money every month. Parents of SPED students have the right to have the IEP reviewed and to monitor whether the student is getting the services that he or she needs. In a school such as Vaux, where the majority of the parents have only a high school education and many receive welfare, they rarely ask questions about what happens in the classroom. Instead, the child is classified as a SPED student for most of his or her school career, and is forced to accept the limited services that the school has to offer, which is extremely inadequate in failing schools.

In the classroom, a SPED student can have the assignments tailored to his/her needs. Last year, in one class of twenty-four students (ranging from grades nine to twelve), I had nine SPED students. Their reading levels ranged from first to sixth grade. In another class of twenty-one students, I had eight SPED students. Their reading levels ranged from Kindergarten to seventh grade. It was extremely challenging to teach to all of these different levels at one time, as well as frustrating because I knew I was not providing the students with the support they needed. There was just not enough of me to go around the room.

In the beginning of the year, George came to class every day. On his IEP, it stated that his reading level was at the first grade. George was MMR, and he had an extremely hard time understanding the material. Instead of doing his assigned work, he would talk to his friends in the class—*nonstop*. I had to interrupt the class frequently to ask him to be quiet, move him to a different seat, or call someone to remove him from the class. By the second quarter, he was skipping three times a week. In addition to addressing him one-on-one, I spoke with his caseworker, I wrote detention slips, and I called his home. His mother did not return my calls. He was frequently assigned to in-house suspension. By the fourth quarter, he was only showing up to class once a week. By May, he never came at all. He was at school, but he would hang out in the lunchroom or the hallways instead of coming to class. Because the law makes it next to impossible to fail a SPED student, I had no other choice than to pass him with the lowest possible grade—a 65 percent. He is free to move on to the next level. How is this system helping him? If he had been in a class with a SPED teacher, who could give him individualized attention, he could have made some progress. Instead, he missed a huge portion of the year and passed anyway. This happens to large numbers of SPED students in urban schools. We are not educating them, because we don't require them to be in a classroom. We are so focused on Least Restrictive Environment (LRE) that they have almost no restrictions at all. In fact, they are free to move about the cabin as they please.

Ashley's IEP stated that she read at the fourth grade level. She had reasonably good attendance for the first quarter. By November, she stopped coming altogether. Instead of coming to class, she would roam the halls or go to the lunchroom. I called her mother, but got no response. I sent home three letters, but never heard from her. I was unable to fail her because she was a SPED student.

In order to fail a SPED student (even if they never come to class), a teacher at our school was required to do the following:

1. Show documentation of all the interventions that have been made (for example: modified work, accommodations in the classroom).
2. Show documentation of all the phone calls and letters to parents, and describe the outcome.
3. Show evidence that you left make-up work for the student with the caseworker.
4. Show documentation that you spoke with the case manager and make a formal request to have the IEP amended.

Most teachers start out the year documenting all of this information, but they very quickly get so bogged down with other duties, that they are unable to keep up with the paperwork. Some teachers are skilled at taking copious notes about students' behavior, daily work ethic, et cetera. One teacher that year commented, "You either teach really well, or document really well. It is hard to do both." Inevitably, the teachers are forced to pass the students anyway because they are told that their paperwork is incomplete. The laws (or administrators) make it so difficult to comply and maintain all the detailed paperwork for the large number of SPED students that these students get passed on.

At the end of the year, one of the math teachers was hell-bent on having all of his documentation in order, so that he could accurately back up his assessments. Many were SPED students who never came to class. He showed me his file-he had documentation for behavior, student-signed contracts to acknowledge the expectations and consequences of their actions, phone calls, and letters to parents, and charts of their scores. His file was complete and detailed. He had to give several of these students failing grades because of truancy and lack of work. When he turned in his grades, he felt confident that he could back up his evaluations with his documentation. The day after he turned in his grades to the office, he received a call from the head of the SPED department. She wanted to see the records to support the failing grades he had given to some students. When he showed the documentation to her, she said, "Yes, but did you send the letters by *certified mail?*"

The teachers were never informed of this detail. She rejected all of his documentation, and passed the students anyway. The SPED specialist told us that the court would require this, and without it, they would never win in front of a judge. Many students are very aware of this, and take advantage of it. All of his students were allowed to pass, many of whom only showed up to class less than ten times and completed five percent of the required work. Teachers can make call after call to a parent, and the parent never calls back. At one meeting, an administrator ask how many of us had made home visits to talk to the parent, suggesting that if we had not, we were not doing all that we could. Consequently, the responsibility and accountability is completely removed from the student and parent, and placed solely on the teacher.

Many teachers, most of whom have worked in the public school system for years, become tired of a system that does not support the teachers' judgment, allows a third party to decide a student's outcome (without ever stepping foot into the class), and passes students whether they do an ounce of work or not. After years of working within a broken system that does not support them as educators, they refuse to complete all of this documentation. In fact, several teachers got into arguments this year because the principal wanted to pass students who almost never came to class. The teachers showed the principal proof, but he insisted that they pass anyway. It is almost as if the system was created to discourage teachers from failing students. What are we teaching the students? "Do a bare minimum of work, you will pass anyway. Or better yet, don't even bother to come to class, you will pass anyway!" They learn at a very young age how to manipulate the system. Even when it comes to attendance, students learn to play the game. After missing ten days of school, a student is considered truant. At this point, they could face going to court. Students know this, so after the ninth day, they come to school so that the ten-day count starts all over again. As long as they attend class once every ten days, they are safe from having to appear in front of the judge.

During the year, I got a visit from the district support person for my content area. She came in unannounced to observe all of the teachers that day. In my class, she witnessed a meltdown of Lawrence, and later that day, I emailed her to explain the frustrations I was experiencing because of the lack of support for him. I told her that many of the SPED students refused to work and were often disruptive. I also explained that there were a large number of students who were so uncomfortable with the level of the material, that they skipped the class and wandered the halls instead. She responded that she would research it, and in the meantime forwarded my e-mail to several people, including the principal.

The next day, I was called in to the principal's office, where he told me that "I had thrown him under the bus," because now people would know that kids at his school skipped class (this affected his reputation and the public's impression of his school). He also said, "You knew what you signed up for," and in a deliberately nice voice, suggested that if I wasn't happy there, I could find another school. (In fact, because he never addressed the issue of the large population of Special Education students at the interview or in training, most of us did not know what we had signed up for.) I responded that I was committed to helping the students, but I was just asking for some support and some tools to help me teach them. In this situation, a teacher knows that the best thing to do is politely agree. If a teacher disagrees, or expresses an opinion that challenges that of the principal, she can expect a surprise visit to the classroom and an unsatisfactory observation, in order to move them out of the building. Retaliation against teachers is a popular management technique for public school principals.

Many of the Special Education students are in the program because they have behavioral problems that can ultimately lead to academic and truancy problems as well. This past year, my sixth period class had an exceptionally large number of emotionally disturbed Special Education students. In a class of twenty-seven students, seventeen of them had IEPs because of emotional problems. Even though I had over ten years of teaching experience at this point, and two and a half in inner-city Philadelphia schools, I was not trained or prepared to teach this many students with emotional issues. In fact, the teacher who had this class before me quit in the middle of the year, because the students' behavior was so outrageous.

When a teacher is teaching this many kids who are lacking in basic skills, it is difficult to follow the school district's curriculum timeline. Good teachers know when to slow down, reteach or teach the concept in a different way if the students are struggling. In a class with so many SPED students, it is extremely challenging to follow the expected pace set by the school district. In this particular class, only around four students consistently paid attention, took notes, and followed the lessons. They were patient as Keinya cursed at me and threatened other students, and I had to stop the lesson to call security. They did their work anyway when I had to stop teaching the day that Zahir and Jarnell started a fistfight that lasted six minutes while I waited for security. Many of the eight students who had emotional issues had spotty attendance. Charles came in the middle of the year from a disciplinary school. He frequently provoked other students, and then would routinely cut class for four days at a time. Shakira would come about once or twice a week. She would walk in, and like many of the female students, never brought a notebook or books, she just carried her purse over her shoulder. She would sit in the back of the room and refuse to work. I would contact the Special Education Liaison about the students' lack of progress. I called the students' homes, and sent letters home to the parents. I asked the SPED teacher who was in charge of the emotionally disturbed students. He came once to observe, but that was it. He was too busy to provide any support.

By law, these students will graduate from high school. If these students were from wealthy suburbs, most likely the parents would make sure that they received the services they need. They would probably be pulled out of regular classes to get tutoring and support. Most parents of poor disadvantaged students do not know their rights. If they did, maybe they would be up at the school complaining to the principal because by law their children are entitled to much more. Instead, they are forgotten in many public inner-city schools. Many of these girls are sexually active (including many of the girls who are MMR), and will go on to have kids of their own while in high school. Six years later, these young mothers will be registering them for kindergarten.

According to an article published by the American-Speech-Language-Hearing Association (ASHA), "it is recognized that adequate development across multiple domains is essential for subsequent school success. It also is important to recognize that when children are exposed to high quality learning opportunities prior to kindergarten, they are less likely to experience school failure and be misidentified as having LD in the early grades."[36] LD has been defined by the National Joint Committee on Learning Disabilities (NJCLD) as a heterogeneous group of disorders manifested by significant difficulties in the acquisition and use of listening, speaking, reading, writing, reasoning, or mathematical abilities. These disorders are intrinsic to the individual, presumed to be due to central nervous system dysfunction, and may occur across the life span."[37] Some children may demonstrate difficulties in early development but may not be at risk for later disabilities. However, specialists say that it is important for parents to take their children for screening and testing, so that if needed, intervention services can be implemented. In poor communities, many parents do not pursue these screening and testing services. Instead, these children are sent to school with undetected learning problems.

There are many environmental factors that can affect a child's development. Many of the possible risk factors are found in poor communities, such as those in inner-city Philadelphia: a family history of spoken and/or written language problems, exposure to environmental toxins or other harmful substances, a limited language exposure in the home, poverty, lack of access to quality pre- and postnatal care, lack of maternal education, lack of high quality learning opportunities, low exposure to rich and varied vocabulary, syntax, and discourse patterns and a lack of access to printed materials.[38] Studies have shown that children living in poverty enter school with poor oral language and vocabulary development. Many of these factors are magnified when a young teen girl gives birth to a child, and raises the child as a single mother. Even though the child may be born healthy, the environment itself can cause many problems for the young child. If these problems are not addressed early on, by the time he or she enters school, the child may possibly be far behind his or her peers in cognitive ability. To compound this problem, if this child enters into a public, underfunded inner-city school, he might never receive the services needed, and will continue his entire school career dangerously behind.

Many of the SPED students in Philadelphia are those who get involved in violent altercations with other students and teachers. According to the *Philadelphia Inquirer*, "From September through February of [2011], 1,628 assaults have been reported in the district, and about 39 percent included at least one special-education student as an offender. The 2007 investigation also found that the district routinely failed to provide services to special-education students, and therefore felt it could not follow through with discipline if the students assaulted a staff member." Without a completely staffed Special Education Department, and sufficient services provided for the large numbers of SPED students, all students in the school will continue to be negatively affected.

Chapter Four

TEACHING IN A BROKEN SYSTEM

n the last few years, our American school system has received more attention in the news, thanks to well-known public figures such as Bill Gates and Michelle Rhee, ex-chancellor of Washington, DC Public Schools. Their criticisms have been heavily focused on teachers. If our schools are years behind other developing countries, they argue, it must be due to our incompetent teachers. Gates believes that "A quarter of our teachers are very good. If you could make all of the teachers as good as the top quarter, the U.S. would soar to the top of that comparison."[39] Who is to judge which teachers are "very good"? Well, certainly not a billionaire who has never been a public school teacher, and who attended a prestigious private high school. The problem is not getting rid of the bad teachers, it is holding on to the good ones.

As a public school teacher, one of the constants I have experienced is working with talented and dedicated teachers. Most teachers go into teaching because they believe in education, love to teach subjects they are passionate about, and to work with children. To criticize the teachers is to criticize our higher education system. A high school teacher today must complete an undergraduate degree and an additional year and a half to two years of a teaching program. In my two-year graduate teaching program, the focus was on learning how to create engaging lessons and fair evaluation systems. Among other things, we learned about education law, the history of education in America, and how to teach within state standards. We had one course on classroom management and one on Special Education. The Special Education class was taught by a woman who taught in one of the wealthiest districts in the state. In fact, the stereotype of her school was that the student parking lot was a sea of Mercedes Benzes and BMWs. She taught us about her students, most of whom had mild learning disabilities or ADHD. Many were on medication that helped improve their ability to focus. They also had very involved upper-middle-class parents who could afford and paid for additional services for their children. This contrasts with my experience in Philadelphia, where many of my students need medication, but don't take it, or their mother took them off it, or they couldn't afford it, or didn't have a parent around to buy it. The result is a large number of students with extremely erratic behavior.

The lack of money for medical services is apparent in other situations too, such as with eyeglasses. Many of my students complain of not being able to see properly and go nine months without ever purchasing glasses. In middle class high schools, students wearing teeth braces is very common, and is something you rarely see in poor inner-city schools. It isn't until you start teaching in an inner city school, that you notice the stark lack of money for services that is taken for granted in other neighborhoods. University level teaching programs need to be designed to prepare teachers better for the reality of public school classrooms. Schools need to educate future teachers on how to effectively address the issues that impede learning such as poverty, emotional and behavioral problems.

In most teaching programs, candidates are required to student teach in a school in the last year of the program. Many programs require student teachers to spend an entire ten-week semester in the classroom. My program required only six weeks of student teaching. There were twenty people in my cohort in graduate school. When the program was over, everyone went their separate ways, finding teaching positions in suburban, rural, or urban schools. In the end, we would all find ourselves in very different environments, depending on the location of the school, and the socioeconomic and cultural backgrounds of the students. But we would all be applying the same concepts we learned in our program, regardless of the cultures, abilities, or socioeconomic status of the students.

During my six weeks as a student teacher, I taught five different English classes. I had to write the lesson plans, teach five classes and was responsible for grading all tests and papers that I assigned during my teaching. It was an immense amount of work. I was student teaching in a public school, but it was an easy assignment compared to the school where I ended up four years later. As a student teacher, I taught all Advanced Placement (AP) classes in an urban public high school. AP classes are taught at a higher level of difficulty, and students can earn college credit for taking them. The students who take these classes are usually higher achieving students and on track to college. They usually have a good work ethic, work well independently, and complete the class assignments and papers. Teaching this population of students is a completely different experience from teaching at a failing school. Needless to say, my student teaching experience did not prepare me for my later years in the Philadelphia urban schools.

If we want to make changes in our failing schools, it is imperative to ensure that teachers are being trained properly in teaching programs. What many educational programs do not do, at least in my experience, is to prepare teachers to teach children in underserved neighborhoods. While we might read novels or essays about poor children from different cultures, this does not prepare us to be able to fully help students who suffer from physical or emotional pain, violence, and hunger. Teachers need practical tools to use in the classroom everyday; how to talk to and teach to a child who is abused, how to develop strategies for students who refuse to do any work, and the list goes on. The success of our students depends on it.

On my Pennsylvania Teacher's Certificate, it states that I am entitled "to practice the art of teaching." The certificate of the Commonwealth of Pennsylvania recognizes that teaching is more accurately described as an art than a science. Those who insist that teaching is an art say that applying educational theories by relating to different personalities, keeping students engaged, building relationships with the students and balancing a curriculum is definitely an art form. Many differ on this; those who believe that teaching is a science say that theory and research build the foundation for what teachers accomplish in the classroom. Teaching requires many skills: having excellent content knowledge, knowing how to manage large groups of adolescents, how to be a counselor, how to work with many different levels of learners in one classroom, how to write creative lessons that both engage and teach. Good teachers have a vision, and are flexible, intelligent, firm, and compassionate. Successful teachers are able to connect with the students, and to develop good relationships that are based on respect and trust. Many of the skills that are needed to be an effective teacher are learned on the job, and are difficult to learn in college teaching courses.

Many reformers today insist that we use student test scores to evaluate teachers' effectiveness. Value-Added Modeling (VAM) is a method to evaluate teachers that is promoted by many corporate reformers today. The method proposes to measure how much a teacher contributes to a child's success. The analysis compares a student's current test scores with the student's test scores of the previous year, as well as to other students in the same grade. The purpose is to isolate how much one teacher contributes to a child's achievement. Critics of the method say that this form of analysis has not been validated. A student's past test scores are used to predict his or her future scores, assuming that students usually score similarly from year to year. The actual score is then compared to the predicted score, and the difference between the two is assumed to be due to the teacher and the school, rather than the student's socioeconomic status or natural ability. That's a lot of assumptions.

Many critics are skeptical, and some have referred to it as "junk science."[40] Researchers for the RAND Corporation, an educational research organization, said, "Although VAM holds great promise, it also raises many fundamental and complex issues. Some of these issues may appear arcane, but the reasonableness of the findings of VAM studies depends on them. If these issues are not adequately addressed, VAM is likely to misjudge the effectiveness of teachers and schools and could produce incorrect generalizations about their characteristics, thus hampering systematic efforts to improve education."[41]

Analyzing test scores is the quickest and most concrete way to measure results. However, the other aspects of the relationship between teacher and students, such as: guiding, inspiring and counseling, and are extremely important in the process, and difficult to measure. To ignore completely the value of these parts of teaching shows a lack of understanding of teaching, especially in schools that serve poor children. By putting so much emphasis on test scores, reformers today seem only to focus on teaching as a science, dismissing and devaluing the art of the craft.

When it comes to teaching, it is extremely difficult to take one theory and apply it to any two classrooms and expect the same result. There are so many outside factors that affect a class, such as the diverse personalities of students, number of lower level learners, behavioral problems, and socioeconomic backgrounds. Learning how to teach in all of these changing conditions is what is impossible to learn in college. In most teaching programs, we learn how to write lessons, but not how to teach to the student who says, "I refuse." We don't learn how to teach to five different reading levels at once. We are not taught what to do when a student tells you to "get the fuck outta my face," or threatens to "fuck you up." These are day-to-day occurrences in a Philadelphia urban classroom. Not only are they challenging moments in the day, they happen repeatedly, and they are stress inducing. Children who attend these schools are under a lot of stress themselves, and they often come to school full of anger.

If standardized tests measure a student's academic achievement, how do you measure all the rest of the educational experience? In a high-performing school, the tests might be a very different assessment than they would be in a turnaround school. In the former, you would be less likely to find issues with truancy, aggressive behavior, suspensions, and expulsions. More children from high achieving schools do the work that is expected of them, understand work ethic, and are goal oriented. In a turn-around school, teachers are still working with kids on attendance, behavioral problems, and the refusal to work. Children from inner city, poor neighborhoods also display behavior that is up to five years behind in maturity level, and lack basic coping skills. In my experience, if a high school student has come through the school system without learning how to complete work, pay attention in class and take school seriously, it is going to take some time to change this behavior. In fact, ten years of attending failing schools may be next to impossible to turn around, which is why mentorships and support programs need to be provided in the early years of elementary school. The students in inner city failing schools are so far behind in cultural capital, that much work is needed to bring them up to the appropriate level. Currently, most public inner city schools do not have the resources to provide additional services. As news of school budget cuts hit the newspapers, we often hear from angry parents. Parents in suburban schools complain about losing art and music programs. In poor inner-city Philadelphia, money is lacking for more basic needs, such as math and reading programs, Special Education teachers, counseling services, and police officers to protect students.

I propose that we have many talented, dedicated teachers in our American school system. Unfortunately, they are working within a system that works against them. For example, in a class of twenty-five eleventh-grade students with ten students that read at an elementary level, how can you expect the teacher to produce results with no support? Improvements in test scores cannot happen as quickly as administrators want them to. When looking at whether a teacher is successful or not, the many changing variables within a classroom need to be taken into account.

Teachers are expected to utilize "Differentiated Instruction," a method of teaching in which teachers tailor their instruction and adjust the curriculum to students' needs rather than expecting students to modify themselves to fit the class. When teaching a specific concept, this involves creating two or three different strategies to teach different groups of students, and creating different activities for each level. It can also mean creating either shorter or longer assignments for students, depending on their ability levels. In fact, we are required to show how we will differentiate our classes on our lesson plans that we submit to the principal each week. Proponents of this method believe that because students have different learning styles and levels, the entire class will benefit from a teacher creating a lesson that addresses all different levels at one time. The reality is though that it is extremely difficult to do this well. Many teachers in public schools in Philadelphia will tell you that the difference in levels is so great, that in this model, one teacher cannot possibly give all the children the attention they need. However, year after year, we are given professional development classes that focus on this concept. Since I have taught in Philadelphia, teachers have never been asked to provide feedback to determine if this is effective or not. Of course, by placing many levels of learners in one class with one-teacher schools saves money. In addition, there is a shortage of Special Education teachers. Last year, one of the SPED teachers was assigned to staff the in-house detention room, instead of teaching. Her talent and special training was wasted on babysitting kids in the detention room. There was no money to hire additional support.

As in many professions, theories change, and fads come and go. I learned more about this as I began to work closely with seasoned teachers, who had anywhere from ten to twenty-five years experience, and had seen many theories and programs go out of favor, only to return under a different name. One example is tracking, which used to be popular years ago, but has since lost its appeal. In the past, students were put into classes based on their ability levels, with the idea that teachers could teach more effectively if all classmates were at similar levels. Then, some educators began to criticize the concept of grouping students of similar socioeconomic status. Some educators felt that tracking could result in a stigmatization of lower track students, and that in this configuration, students were often not challenged to achieve at higher levels. In recent years, educators have favored a more inclusive model, which is believed by many to be a more equitable environment for students. A common thought today is that a classroom that represents different cultures, backgrounds and learning levels, promotes a sharing of knowledge and transference of skills between students. As a graduate student working towards my Masters of Education, this concept made a lot of sense to me. After all, wasn't a democratic learning environment just that, giving students from diverse educational, economic, cultural, racial backgrounds equal opportunity, and an opportunity to learn from each other? In theory, it seems plausible that lower level learners can learn from higher-level learners, white students from students of color and higher-level learners could become teachers of those who are behind.

As is the case with many educational theories, putting them to use in the classroom is very different from reading about them in a textbook. No one can predict the dynamic of a classroom. There are most likely anywhere from twenty-five to thirty different family histories, learning styles and varying levels of stress in the students' lives. Then add poverty to the mix. In my graduate program, which I completed in 2009, we never studied nor discussed how to deal with the effects of poverty on children in the classroom. Yet, the failing schools that need good teachers are largely located in poverty-stricken areas. It isn't until a teacher has his or her own classroom does he start to understand what works and what doesn't, and what adjustments need to be made to the lesson plans and curriculum to create the best learning environment for each student. Precious time is lost when teachers receive no training on effective strategies for children in poverty. Teaching programs need to better prepare and train teachers to work with failing students. You can be a great teacher; dedicated, focused, highly educated in your content area, and have great classroom management. But this is not preparation enough for one teacher to effectively help poor students. One teacher cannot possibly address all of these students' needs.

The best environment would be a cooperative school, where a team of people is readily available to work with both teachers and students. Teachers should be able to refer students to tutors, counselors, and mentors to give students extra time and guidance outside of the classroom. For example, even though I am always available to tutor students after school, few kids take advantage of it. If a teacher has a student who is struggling with a specific subject, there should be a mandatory tutoring program in place to help them. When students are having problems at home, it would be helpful to have a team of counselors who are trained to work with these issues. Schools with high numbers of poor students need extra services to help them to be successful. A collaborative school would be one that has counselors who are trained to work with poor children, with learning and emotional problems. These specialists would be open and available to receive students who are referred to them by teachers who detect a need for more personalized attention. As it is now (in the schools where I have worked), if student cannot function at the appropriate level, he or she is left in the general education classroom, does little work, and gets lost in classes that are too difficult for their skill level.

All over the United States, as the student population has become more diverse, the teaching force has become less so. According to a 2009 report, in Philadelphia, 87 percent of the students in public schools are minority, two thirds of which are black, while less than 34 percent of the teachers are non-white.[42] Many believe that minority students benefit from having teachers of the same background. There is no doubt that if a teacher has grown up in a similar environment as his students, there will be a greater level of understanding of the issues that get in the way of learning. When Superintendent Ackerman announced her program, "Imagine Greatness," part of the plan was to increase the percentage of minority teachers to 51 percent by 2014. The district's Chief Talent Development Officer claimed that, "Students of color need to see that role model and understand that what they see in front of them is attainable and that they can get there with a mentor and support system." Unfortunately, according to *The Notebook*, "A big factor in the shortage of black teachers is the under-representation of African Americans in colleges of education. One teacher commented, "There is an achievement gap that runs deep and follows you throughout school."[43]

Formal observations of teachers are scheduled ahead of time with the principal. In Philadelphia, there is supposed to be a pre-observation meeting, an observation of the entire class hour, a written evaluation and a post-observation meeting to discuss the principal's findings. There is a standard twelve-page form that is to be filled out by the administrator. The main categorizes of critique are: planning and preparation, classroom environment, instruction, and professionalism. The quality of the feedback depends on the involvement of the principal and his commitment to the teachers. It is very apparent when a principal respects the work of teachers. He schedules the observation time and he shows up. Most teachers welcome an open discussion about our craft, and the students we are teaching. Very often a principal will schedule a time to observe a teacher, then just not bother to show up, or even call or e-mail to reschedule. The teacher has prepared all the requested and required materials for the principal, and the administrators are too busy to reschedule. In any corporate setting, if an employee did not show up to a meeting, it would be considered unprofessional. But this is the norm in the public school system, and it demonstrates the lack of respect and regard for teachers. The time that I did meet with an administrator after an observation (once in the last three years), the meeting was brief, and if there was a suggestion, it was not followed up with professional development. The other meetings were never rescheduled or were cancelled by the principal. If a principal suggests that a teacher could work on their discussion techniques, it would be helpful if there were training or suggested reading, or similar guidance. Usually, principals do not have time to discuss what they saw when they observed you, so there is little feedback.

I have heard principals make the comment to teachers on more than one occasion, "We don't provide on the job training. You should know these things by now." Yet if there is a need for improvement, schools need to respond with coaching, not a tearing down of a teacher's performance, to create a positive and supportive work environment, one that values quality teaching. Instead, many principals are distant, unapproachable and (in every high school I have worked in) create a hostile and punitive environment for the teachers. This dynamic is so harmful to the school and students that many teachers leave at the end of the year.

Often the administration offers professional development classes or seminars on topics that are neither applicable nor relevant to our specific school. At the end of the year at Vaux, we had two sessions on multiple learning styles, a topic that we had all learned in college. Though an interesting topic, this did not address the more urgent skills we needed help with. The principal could have organized seminars on more useful topics; teachers in poor urban schools need to be trained in how to work with kids with anger issues, how to teach SPED students, understanding poverty, communicating with students, and talking to kids with family issues to name a few. These are more pressing topics that impede learning and prevent student success.

During the required six weeks to two months of student teaching, the student teacher is in a classroom with the mentor teacher, and while the student teacher usually teaches most of the classes during this internship, the mentor teacher is there to diffuse any behavior issues. New teachers could benefit from more time in a classroom so that they could get more hands on experience. Little can prepare you for teaching in a failing inner city school. Complaints about teachers' classroom management skills are common from principals, yet I have never seen an individual school offer training or coaching for teachers who struggle with it. In an urban failing school, it is inevitable that there will be behavior issues. These schools are often labeled as "persistently dangerous." Just as Vaux is, they are often located in drug-ridden neighborhoods, where violence is prevalent. A lot of valuable class time is wasted when teachers have to deal with angry students who don't want to learn. If a principal is more concerned with making his number of incidents appear low, he will be looking for a quicker solution, such as hiding information, not methods to solve school behavior-management issues.

Every teacher knows that there are numerous, ever changing factors that affect the success of a class. A teacher can teach one lesson to a first period class with great success (engaged students, high participation, and level of understanding). The bell rings, and in walks second period. A completely different group of kids; maybe they are not in the mood to learn, they are disruptive, uncooperative and the lesson is not successful. Student-to-student dynamic, different learning levels, as well as the number of kids with behavioral problems can all affect how a class operates on any given day. A teacher instructs to the group, but meanwhile each individual has his or her own set of familial issues, self-identity questions, and dose of the expected teen-age strife. In the life of a child in poverty, such as a student at Vaux High School, you can add to that natural turmoil: a parent is in jail, a mom is a drug addict, a dad left home yesterday, a boyfriend was shot, or a sister was locked up.

At Vaux, when the afternoon bell rang, few students took any work home. For these children, when school is out, they don't think about it until the next day. If you ask them if a teacher assigns homework, students will say no, but ask the teacher to see the grade book, and you will see rows and rows of zeros that represent the students' refusal to do the work. I have always assigned homework in my classes. At Vaux, the students knew it represented 15 percent of their final grade. After two months, I realized that only 20 percent of the kids were turning in any work. I decided to give them time in class to work on it instead. I wanted them to get the needed practice, and they refused to do it otherwise.

These are adjustments you have to make in failing schools. In a middle class school, or school where students have academic goals, students react to receiving poor grades, and make the connection between effort extended and grades received. In failing schools, there is an attitude that "I don't care, and I can do what I damn please." Many parents don't expect their children to work hard, and they don't ask questions about their work. How can we change this attitude towards education? Perhaps schools need to give it more immediate value to the parents and the students. Some successful schools actually require parents to sign an agreement to support the child at home when they enroll their child. This is not done in public schools.

When the layoffs happened at Vaux High School, there were so many teachers with only one to two years' experience, that many of them lost their jobs due to lack of seniority. Many of the younger, inexperienced teachers bring something very valuable to schools that can't be measured in a test. They bring a fresh outlook, new ideas, and great energy. Many people oppose the seniority system as it exists now. In the case of layoffs, the teachers with more years in the district get to hold on to their jobs, and the newest are the first to go. It is a common opinion today that "teachers in high poverty schools generally have less experience and are of lower quality than teachers in wealthy districts where students already achieve at higher levels."[44] In my experience, less time in the classroom does not automatically mean lower quality. If students in wealthy districts already achieve at high levels, their socioeconomic status, parent involvement and the cultural capital that they bring to school contribute hugely to these successes. It is immensely more difficult to teach in urban failing schools, where kids tell you to "go fuck yourself" when you ask them to please open their book. There is no comparison between the two environments. One must analyze the entire picture. Do the classes in wealthy districts have 50 percent Special Education students? Are 30 percent of the students reading five years below grade level? This is the student population in inner city Philadelphia. To ignore this is dishonest and wrong.

Large numbers of underachieving students are minorities. Teachers from middle class backgrounds come into inner-city schools and have difficulties relating to, and understanding students' coping mechanisms. In my experience, students who come from disadvantaged backgrounds cope with stress by getting angry. They are angry because there are problems at home. They are angry because they have to come to school, they are angry because their electricity was shut off, they are angry because their father left them, they are angry because they do not understand the teacher's lesson. So they react in the only way they know how—with aggravation and often rage. Administrators in Philadelphia are largely African American, which should be a huge asset to teachers. These educators could initiate training for teachers in the schools. Instead, in many schools, there is an attitude of hostility towards white teachers and they are quick to criticize them for not understanding the culture of the children. Administrators have a great opportunity to use their own knowledge to educate teachers and provide them with tools needed to help our students. All too frequently, instead of working together with the teachers, the principal and other administrators are at odds with one another.

In Philadelphia schools, more than 85 percent of the student population lives below the poverty line. Critics say that schools with high rates of poverty have a lower number of "highly qualified" teachers and a higher turnover of teachers. In Philadelphia's low performing schools, one in five teachers has less than two years experience, and many schools lose up to 40 percent of their teachers each year.[45] Much of this is because the number of safe schools in Philadelphia is low, so teachers who get hired into a good school with low violence stay for years, and do not transfer. On the other hand, teachers in violent schools have a high burnout rate, because it is extremely stressful and can be harmful to one's physical and mental health.

We must be careful with the term, "highly qualified." It is a term that is determined by certification in the subject area and level of education. Many teachers come to the district from other states, and while working towards their state specific certification (which usually means taking a PRAXIS test (that tests knowledge of the content area), and providing all documentation from the universities that the teacher attended), the district will allow teachers to teach with an "emergency certification." Other teachers who use the emergency certification are those who are in the process of being certified, but don't complete the test by September, and TFA teachers, who have not completed a certification program. One of our language teachers was a good example of how this term is misused. She had two master's degrees, and nine years teaching experience, had been certified in another state, but was waiting for her new certification. The principal still referred to her as not being "highly qualified" because she did not have the state certification yet. The PRAXIS tests are the same nationwide, but states sometimes differ in terms of what tests they require. Teachers with less experience get lower salaries, so they cost the district less. TFA teachers are paid less than regular teachers are, so for a school with a tight budget, hiring from these two groups can save money.

It is not accurate to assume that just because a teacher has not completed the certification yet, that they are not successful teachers. Many of the newer teachers bring valuable talent and dedication to teaching. If more schools functioned collaboratively, by establishing counseling, mentoring, and tutoring programs so that students had more resources to guide them to academic success, then the newer teachers would more likely develop their skills at a quicker pace. As many schools function today, newer teachers experience many months of frustration and ineffectiveness because they are learning on the job with little support in the classroom. It is well known that most teachers are not as effectual in the first year because it takes a year or so for a teacher to figure out best practices and strategies. If schools only measure a teacher's success by test scores, then maybe these teachers will not produce the same results as more seasoned teachers. We must acknowledge the value of new teachers for their interest and commitment level, which can be extremely beneficial to kids in high poverty schools.

On the last day of school, in her speech to the entire staff, our principal last year said, "Some of you weren't meant to be teachers, so you should re-evaluate what you want to do." We just sat there in disbelief. How could a leader of teachers be so negative? By that point, many of the teachers had personally felt her hostility all year long, had already found jobs elsewhere, and were happy to be leaving. Why is there a high turnover of teachers in failing schools? In Philadelphia, it is increasingly difficult to obtain a teaching position in the suburbs because jobs are scarce. Teachers hold on to jobs in good schools with high levels of parental involvement, more support, and little violence. In big cities like Philadelphia, the alternative is working in the city schools, which are dangerous and underfunded, and have little to no support, all elements that make for difficult working conditions. Add to that the poor leadership in administrations and many teachers do not last long. In the school district newspaper, *The Notebook,* Philadelphia teachers responded to an article about high teacher turnover.

One teacher commented, "Here's a cheap and easy way to keep teachers in high poverty (and any other) schools: Hire principals who are real leaders, not just administrators. No matter where a school is located or who its students are, when the principal cultivates an *esprit de corps* among its teachers by standing by them, communicating with them, encouraging them and showing them consistent appreciation, those teachers will stay. I've taught at a dozen schools over the years, and most of them are run by colorless, toneless, sometimes antagonistic administrators, rather than leaders who inspire loyalty."

Another teacher added, "If the district spent more time on hiring captains that knew how to sail their ships forward instead of trying to intimidate the crews they would have a hell of a lot more successful voyages to brag about. A school full of good teachers can't turn around a school run by a deadbeat principal.[46] It seems to be a common problem in Philadelphia schools that principals have difficulties with building and maintaining good teams of teachers. Antagonistic relationships between the principal and teaching staff is very common, in fact I have seen it at all of the five schools where I have taught.

Many principals only seem to know one way of managing—in a punitive environment. Poor relationships between the principal and teachers means there is little trust, appreciation, and value of teachers. Without this important relationship in place, teachers who are already beaten down by the aggressive and violent behavior of the students, begin to feel it from the top also. Very quickly, there is a drop in teacher morale, and the energy and level of caring plummets. I have seen this happen as early as December and January of a school year. Teachers get discouraged, and lose their desire to work for the team. This is akin to a football coach trying to lead a group of players who feel disrespected and unappreciated. Would the players want to follow the coach's plays? In these schools, there is little to no communication except for the "write ups" that are dropped off in a teacher's mailbox. "Write ups" are often retaliatory and unfounded. At one school last year, four teachers were written up when they used the school gym after work to exercise, failing to ask the principal's permission first.

Many successful companies understand the benefits of exercise to the health of their employees. At this particular Philadelphia high school, this was seen as insubordination, which frightened the principal into disciplining her teachers. It did nothing but contribute to the already negative relationship that the principal had created. Seven of those teachers ended up leaving that year, after they had worked tirelessly to help the students to reach AYP eight years in a row. She also moved several teachers out of the building by use of a common tactic. If a principal wants to get rid of a math teacher for example, she will rewrite the job description as an impossible combination of two certifications, such as math and French, so that the teacher is no longer eligible, and she can force them out.

The 100 best places to work in the United States have one thing in common: trust. These companies are all places where employees "trust the people they work for, have pride in what they do, and enjoy the people they work with. Having this kind of trust also decreases costs by lowering turnover (best companies typically have a voluntary turnover of 9 percent or *less*) and lowering resistance to change. Surprisingly, it also lowers health care costs: Employees who feel trusted—and trust their companies in return—tend to have healthier lives outside of work because they leave work *at work,* leaving them with more to give to their personal life (family and community). The best companies to work for also motivate, empower, listen, thank, develop, care, celebrate and share."[47]

It is unfortunate that more principal programs don't instill these ideas. Especially, in the field of education, where teachers work in a high stress environment in the classroom, many principals do not understand how important it is to provide a positive working environment, and to have their teachers behind them. Instead, principals don't seem to care that teachers are against them, the building becomes divided and stays that way all year, which results in lost opportunities of collaboration and progress. Over and over again, a common complaint about principals is that they are "unapproachable." Teachers retreat, feel unvalued, many decide half way through the year that they are not coming back, and they lose their motivation to be good teachers. In these schools, teacher absences are high, and students lose valuable learning time with substitute teachers. Obviously, the students suffer most in these situations from the loss of teachers. It's not about getting rid of bad teachers, as many reformers today want us to believe. It is about valuing and supporting the good ones we have. Good companies recognize talent, and want to keep it. Poorly managed schools push talent right out the door.

U.S. Secretary of Education Arne Duncan speaks to this when he says, "A lot of other countries have done this in a much more thoughtful and strategic way than we have. We must reverse the flow of talent away from the communities and schools that need the most help—getting that great talent to come and then stay. We must devote resources to a great math teacher, a great science teacher, a literacy coach who might be a good principal …We need to create a great cohort of folks with a great principal to support you and help build the community you need."[48] In all five of the high schools where I have worked, there *was* "great talent, a great bunch of peers, a great cohort of folks." What was missing was support-for the students and teachers, so many teachers ended up leaving, either to another school or back to corporate America.

If a teacher accepts a position in an urban failing school, they soon find themselves in front of a class of thirty students, the majority of whom have been raised in violent, poor neighborhoods, come to school angry and defensive, have very little interest in learning, and communicate the only way they know how—aggressively and in a confrontational manner. Young people who grow up in violent neighborhoods learn to be on the defensive, and they learn from those around them how to verbalize their needs and desires-by demanding, yelling and insulting others. No matter how talented they are, this can be a huge shock to teachers who did not grow up in similar neighborhoods. In my high school last year, some of the teachers discussed how we a needed to offer a class to our students on basic communication. Many students do not know how to express themselves effectively, either with other students or with teachers. These are huge roadblocks to learning.

I cannot count the number of times when I asked a student to sit down, please be quiet or to start working, the responses were variations of, "Shut the fuck up, I don't fucking want to, I'm going to fuck you up, or I'm gonna slap the shit outta you." Children who have no problem looking at an adult and saying these things, do not respond to regular modes of discipline. These children have been deeply hurt by their environments, or their families, or both. Even knowing this, it is extremely difficult (especially if the teacher has never worked in an inner city school) to know how to respond to these children. A natural and common response is one of anger and disgust. "How can this child dare talk to me this way?" Many teachers want to punish the child, and this is the most common outcome—a detention, or a visit to the vice principal. Some schools in Philadelphia are experimenting with alternative, more collaborative methods of discipline (such as Restorative Practices), but this is new and most schools still employ the "detention or suspension" scenario. What happens is trouble-students are suspended repeatedly, and miss weeks and weeks of learning time.

Most often, the student is assigned a punishment (detention) or just a talking to, and then is sent back to class. Ten minutes later, the child who just told the teacher to "shut the fuck up" is back in his or her class. The teacher feels immediately disrespected by the administration, because they are not taking the threat seriously. Few administrators know how to handle the violent behavior either. One day, an eleventh grader in the hallway was told by the principal to get to class. He looked to her and said, "Shut the fuck up, you stupid midget bitch!" She just turned and walked away. A few weeks later, when one of the vice-principals told a young sophomore student to get to his class because he was late, the student told him, "Suck my dick!" The vice principal did nothing. But, according to our Secretary of Education, a "master teacher" would know how to handle this. Will this master teacher be trained in how to deal with kids who threaten to fuck them up? I hope so. These are not empty threats either. I know of three teachers who have been attacked by students in Philadelphia Schools. One lost the use of his eye for a year.

My teaching experience has been in high schools. I have never taught elementary school children, so I cannot speak from firsthand experience. I do know about the home lives of many of my students though, and the truth about what these children experience at home is alarming. Often small children are forced to act in the role of parent at a very young age. When they grow up in dysfunctional homes, their futures are far from bright. When Rita, who was sixteen when I taught at Vaux, had to take time off from school to take her crack-addicted mother to the doctor, she told me a little about her home life. She was the only person in their household who was functional enough to care for her mother. Her father was not around, and her little brother was in the first grade. Rita was emotionally unstable and according to her IEP, MMR. Because her mother had been on drugs for years, she had grown up in a home where essentially, there was no adult figure. She did the best she could and graduated at the end of the year. Subsidies need to be put in place to support these young children in the early years. We cannot wait until they get into the high schools, because years and years of damage cannot be reversed easily. We cannot turn our backs on these kids and give up, and we cannot waste time pointing fingers at teachers, while ignoring the horrible effects of poverty and serious health problems on these children's educations and possibility for a better future.

Let's refocus our efforts to equip students with the tools to achieve. So many children come to school without the basics: parental support, a loving and nurturing home or a nutritious diet. But if we are as serious as we say we are about creating a better national school system, then we must look honestly and realistically at what is impeding progress. We know that there has been a persistent achievement gap in the schools for years. Minority children who are not performing well in school come from predominantly poor communities. Teachers believe in education, and they believe in bettering themselves as educators. Provide them with the knowledge about how to help poor children. Educate them about the best strategies to teach disadvantaged children, and support them in the classrooms.

The PISA survey, conducted every three years by the Organization for Economic Co-operation and Development (OECD) compares fifteen year olds in different countries in reading, math, and science. Finland has ranked at or near the top in all three competencies on every survey since 2000. In Finland, teachers are not evaluated based on test scores. In the United States, the Race to the Top initiative invites states to compete for federal dollars using tests and other methods to measure teachers, a philosophy that would not fly in Finland. "I think, in fact, teachers would tear off their shirts," said Timo Heikkinen, a Helsinki principal with twenty-four years of teaching experience. "If you only measure the statistics, you miss the human aspect."[49] It is interesting to look at the manner in which the Finnish approach and value education. "In 1979, it became a requirement that every teacher earn a fifth-year master's degree in theory and practice at one of eight state universities, which is paid for by the state. Teachers are valued in the Finnish society, and are seen as having equal status with doctors and lawyers. Applicants began flooding teaching programs, not because the salaries were so high but because autonomy and respect made the job attractive. In 2010, some 6,600 applicants vied for 660 primary school training slots, according to Sahlberg. One Finnish principal said, "We have our own motivation to succeed because we love the work," said Louhivuori. "Our incentives come from inside."[50]

Finland does not have a history of racial discrimination like the United States. In fact, the rate of poverty is much lower than the United States, closer to 2 percent. This is one factor that makes a comparison of the two countries challenging. Decades of racial inequity and discrimination in the United States. have had a profound effect on the success of our minority children. In Finland, however, there is an awareness of the importance of support for children at a young age. It's almost unheard of for a child to show up hungry or homeless. The country provides three years of maternity leave and subsidized day care to parents and preschool for all five year olds. In addition, the state subsidizes parents, paying them around 150 euros each month for every child until the age of seventeen. Ninety-seven percent of six year olds attend public preschool, where children begin some academics. Schools provide food, medical care, counseling, and taxi service if needed, and student health care is free.

One of the most difficult things in many failing schools is creating an environment of cooperation between administrators and teachers. Though it is difficult to point to one reason for this lack of teamwork, I can attest to its detrimental effect on the teaching staff. It could possibly be due to the ways schools are structured, that principals have too much responsibility. Administrators have to manage budgets, deal with parents, and scrutiny from the district, in addition to leading the teachers, so having to deal with the teachers might be considered burdensome. Whatever the reason may be, if relationships between professionals in schools break down, so will the educational system within the school. In

Finland, teachers are held with high esteem, and their jobs are seen as an essential part of a modern, functioning society. In addition, there are no private schools in Finland, all Finnish children attend public schools. All American children deserve and should receive a free and excellent education.

Chapter Five

HIGH STAKES TESTING VERSUS REALITY

The No Child Left Behind Act of 2001 (NCLB) supported standards-based education reform, based on the idea that by establishing common high standards, gains could be measured, and closely monitored. NCLB required all states to develop tests that evaluate basic skills, and to administer them to all students at specific grade levels in order to receive federal school funding. Every state was responsible to create their own test, and adopt three levels of outcomes such as: basic, proficient, and below basic. All public schools that received federal funding were required to administer tests to students from third to eighth grades, and in high schools in reading and math. In Pennsylvania, according to the Department of Education website, "The annual Pennsylvania System of School Assessment (PSSA) is a standards-based, criterion-referenced assessment used to measure a student's attainment of the academic standards while also determining the degree to which school programs enable students to attain proficiency of the standards. Every Pennsylvania student in grades three through eight and grade eleven is assessed in reading and math. Every Pennsylvania student in grades five, eight, and eleven is assessed in writing. Every Pennsylvania student in grades four, eight, and eleven is assessed in science."[51]

One of the most controversial expectations of NCLB was that "all students would be proficient in reading and math by the year 2014." As Diane Ravitch stated, "The goal set by Congress of 100 percent proficiency by 2014 is an aspiration; it is akin to a declaration of belief. Yes, we believe that all children can learn and should learn. But as a goal, it is utterly out of reach."[52] Yet, for years now, schools nationwide have been working under these incredibly unrealistic goals. NCLB also states that all schools must prove gains in test scores and make Annual Yearly Progress (AYP). If not, schools were categorized as a School In Need of Improvement (SINI), and ran the risk of eventually being restructured (as occurred at Vaux High School), turned over to the state or to a private charter school.

In order to be eligible for federal funding, the schools must be evaluated, and students must be tested. Educators have criticized high stakes testing for years, for its inaccurate representation and the waste of time spent "teaching to the test." In English, science and math classes especially, teachers are forced to drop everything in their planned curriculum, and use class time to prepare their students. This can last for months leading up to the tests, depending on the school. The principal decides when teachers will start preparing the students for the PSSAs and it is closely monitored. In Pennsylvania, students usually take the PSSAs in March. (Starting in 2013, the School District of Philadelphia switched to a different state assessment called the Keystone exams). Last year, our school also required all teachers to conduct a writing test prep day one day a week for the whole year, which left us with only four days to cover our specific curriculum. One Philadelphia English teacher commented:

> PSSA test prep takes up time in the classroom that could otherwise be devoted to quality instruction. For example, students are repeatedly taught specific strategies to implement

during the PSSA instead of being taught real reading and writing skills that they can use in the real world. Many of the strategies that students are taught for the test are only valuable as a tool for the PSSA. PSSAs fail to assess student progress for a myriad of reasons. To name just a few, students are assessed based only on math and English skills, therefore diminishing the value of many other important skills and contents. Also, students' scores from one year are measured against the scores of a completely different student group from the previous year to see if progress has been made. This is blatantly inaccurate. Students are not measured based on their own progress. Next, the concept of 100 percent proficient and advanced at any point is just impossible. The population tested includes special education students that cannot be expected to attain proficient and advanced scores. How do these tests affect our students? Less funding for those that are already underfunded, less focus in real world instruction and twenty-first century skills and a general disenfranchisement with our educational system on the part of our students.

Another problem with such a strong focus on testing is cheating. With so much money riding on student scores, a shocking number of schools have been accused of cheating; manipulating scores, helping students, even erasing wrong answers. I have never seen this in any of the five schools where I have taught, but I have felt the pressure from the principals to push the kids hard when it comes to testing. Cheating has been reported in cities such as Atlanta, Washington, DC, Los Angeles, Philadelphia, and Houston, to name a few. Why would educators manipulate test scores? If school budgets are constantly cut, principals see the federal funds as one of the only ways to pay for programs, not just special enrichment programs such as sports, music and dance, but money for the basics. In a failing school, this can mean paying police officers in the hallways to protect the students and teachers and paying teachers' salaries. Resources such as textbooks are not even discussed. In the last two years at the failing schools where I worked, I did not have a complete set of textbooks for all of my students. When it comes to resources such as learning materials, teachers just don't even ask anymore. It is just accepted that if you want something for your students, you buy it with your own money.

Interestingly enough, you rarely hear teachers complain about the lack of textbooks. Because there are so many other pressing issues in failing schools—such as safety and support resources for the students. At a staff meeting in February of last year, our principal told the teachers, "We have no money left in our school budget. Period." In July 2012, after a year of budget deficit woes in the School District of Philadelphia, it was reported that the deficit had grown from $218 million to somewhere between $255 and $282 million. Our public schools do not have money to run the buildings. Today, reformers want to convert public schools to privately-run charter schools and invest in online schools. What will happen to the public schools when money is diverted to charter schools? They will continue to crumble in the poor neighborhoods, and many, many children will lose out on an education. For large numbers of these children, the system has already failed them, because after high school they do not pursue further training.

Many of the poor remain poor. Disadvantaged children come to school several years behind most middle class students. They quickly drop further behind, as schools are unable to provide basic support for learning disabilities. Schools need money to run special programs. If we don't address these immediate needs, many children will never catch up. Teachers who oppose funding for charter schools see the negative results of underfunded schools every day. These poor children in public schools will not benefit from new charter schools, mostly because their parents are not equipped to research options, and will continue to send their children to neighborhood public schools. The money that goes to privatized charter schools takes away from these public schools that are desperately in need.

It's 2013, and the new corporate reformers continue to push for high stakes testing, not only to assess students, but also to evaluate teachers, and to hold teachers accountable. Accountability has become a popular word in educational reform in the last few years, and it is focused on teachers in the classroom. Corporate reformers, such as Bill Gates, Michelle Rhee, and Arne Duncan believe that they stand for positive change: high-stakes testing to evaluate teachers, the elimination of tenure and seniority, funding for charter schools, and merit pay are some of the more important points of new reform.

Those who oppose their ideas are considered to be "defending the status quo." In other words, those of us who support the unions, collective bargaining, and increased public school funding must want our schools to remain the same. In fact, most teachers understand very well that reform is needed, but we also see how corporate reformers are totally missing the mark when it comes to helping children to be successful. Applying private business ideas to public schools will not work. Our public education system has become more and more about running a business, and I am afraid that many people forget to focus on the children, and what they need today to become more successful students. There is no time for experimenting with whether merit pay works. What about the children who attend high schools today? The longer we wait to provide them with the tools they need, the more kids who will graduate without an education. Students like Robert, Tyreek, and Dashanique need help today.

Corporate reformers don't seem to believe that experience in teaching has value. One of the most baffling ideas that has come out of corporate reform is the contradiction over the value of teaching. From this standpoint, reformers say that we should make teaching more accessible to more people, to attract a better pool of teachers. On Republican candidate Mitt Romney's website, he supported this concept, when he stated that we need to, "eliminate unnecessary certification requirements that discourage new teachers. For instance, the federal "highly qualified teacher" requirement, while well intentioned, only serves to reinforce hurdles that prevent talented individuals from entering the teaching profession in the first place." [53]

This comment is inaccurate. I don't believe that the qualification requirements for teachers are too stringent for teacher candidates. Talented and qualified individuals are not afraid of getting a college degree and certification to enter a profession. If an educator is going to teach a particular subject, he should have the degree that proves he is a specialist in that area. Bill Gates, whose foundation has spent millions on educational research, believes that both experience and master's degrees show no bearing on whether someone will be a great teacher or a mediocre one. And yet, Gates believes that having a great teacher is the only way to bring up student test scores. According to Gates, we need great teachers, but they are better if they do not have experience or higher degrees.

Gates has also spoken out about class size, saying that large classes of thirty to thirty-two students do not negatively affect learning. Gates proposes removing caps on class size, and offering teachers financial incentives to teach more students. "If you look at something like class sizes going from twenty-two to twenty-seven, and paying that teacher a third of the savings, and you make sure it's the effective teachers you're retaining, by any measure, you're raising the quality of education when you do that."[54] Meanwhile, Gates' own two children reportedly go to private schools, which cost approximately $25,000 per year, and have class sizes of seventeen students or less. Gates believes in putting a "great teacher" in front of every classroom. Increased class size means less individualized attention for each student. Students who need extra help with a new concept, students who are struggling with writing, math, or any other subject do not get the attention they need in big classes. In a fifty-minute class period, one teacher cannot possibly spend enough quality time with thirty students. High achieving students are more independently motivated and self-sufficient. In failing schools, or any other school that has a wide range of learners, those who have difficulty with the material do not get the attention they need in a large class. This would be especially detrimental in schools with students of poverty, who rarely seek out tutoring, nor get help at home. At this time, I teach classes with thirty to thirty-three students, I assign homework four nights a week, which means I correct 600 assignments per week, and when I have to correct multiple-page tests, that time doubles. If I had forty students, as Gates has proposed, I would be even more bogged down with work, and I'm not sure I could be that "great teacher." It takes hours to create, prepare and plan good lessons. Even great teachers need sleep. However, if my class sizes were increased, I am sure that I would somehow find the time.

Evidence supports the idea that teachers with more experience are more effective than new teachers in the classroom. One problem is that even when teachers get a few years of experience under their belt, they still feel so overwhelmed and under supported, that many decide to leave the profession altogether. If schools had better collaborative support programs for teachers, and found administrations more open to helping teachers become better educators, these newer teachers would stay in teaching. It doesn't make sense to replace experienced teachers with new ones, if it is well documented that newer teachers take time to get up to speed. Build up and support the existing teachers we have. It has been my experience that teachers have strengths and weaknesses, just like in all professions. Most teachers are very motivated to polish and improve their craft. With a well-designed support system, made up of seasoned teachers, experts on poverty, and open and honest communication, I am confident that teachers would take full advantage.

In addition to not believing that experience in the classroom matters, corporate reformers propose that it would be easier to get rid of ineffective teachers if there were no unions. Teacher unions support teachers with experience and seniority, which reformers are convinced gets in the way of progress. I do not see the correlation that corporate reformers try to draw between years in the classroom and poor student performance. Just as in all professions, there are excellent, mid level and weak teachers. Investing in the teachers who need help in certain areas makes more sense, especially when they are already dedicated to the kids, and most likely have established relationships with them. Unions do protect employees and require a much lengthier process to fire employees than is customary in private companies. However, to propose that this is the reason that students are not excelling in public schools is ludicrous. The unions fight for the teachers, who are on the front lines with the students. Unions tend to be more understanding of teachers' needs in the classroom. A common complaint of corporate reformers is that unions protect adults, and don't put the needs of the children first. This is simply not true. Our working environment is their learning environment. You cannot easily separate the two.

In a speech to the American Federation of Teachers in 2010, Gates stated, "There is an expanding body of evidence that says the single most decisive factor in student achievement is excellent teaching."[55] Most of us will agree that having a good teacher is extremely important. But if you take an excellent teacher out of a thriving suburban school and place him into a failing inner city school, you cannot expect the same results. I have taught in failing schools and I have taught in two "special admit" schools. I am the same teacher. In all of my teaching jobs, I arrive at 6:30 AM, leave around 5 PM, and work eight to ten hours on the weekend. I offer tutoring, stay after school to help students, and spend hours preparing my lessons, correcting tests and homework. In the special admit schools, the students are very self-sufficient, and large percentages go on to college. Teachers can assign homework, and students complete it without complaining. The percentage of Special Education students is under 5 percent. In the special admit school, large percentages of students receive As and Bs, because they study, pay attention in class, and are supported by their families who expect them to work hard. I get much better results because the student population consists of kids who are motivated and goal oriented. When I give a test in a failing school, many students don't show up, and large numbers fail. In fact, the problem with truancy in failing schools is very serious. At both Promise Academies where I worked, in a class of twenty-eight students, I could expect six to eight students to be absent every day. Missing class time has a grave effect on a student's ability to be successful, especially in a school where students who return to class after being absent for several days do not bother to make up missed work-they just continue to fall behind. This makes a big impact on the class when you are expected to follow a curriculum time line. When large numbers of students miss classes, they cannot perform well on tests. In addition, it is difficult to move the class at a good pace, because you must spend time reteaching concepts.

As Gates went on to say during his speech, "Great teaching is the centerpiece of a strong education; everything else revolves around it." Teachers need to be supported, and the environment must be one that is conducive to learning. He says that parents and administrators "have greater obligations-to support better teaching."[56] Yes, parents have obligations, but it is time to face the reality about the parents at failing schools. Many of the parents are poor, and barely graduated from high school themselves. They do not value education, and do not help their kids with homework, monitor their school grades, or even make sure their kids get to school on time. If we want to have parent involvement, we need to be able to fund a team of people to work with the parents, or a team of counselors who can act in place of the parents in the schools. Gates further elaborated, "We have to make sure that teachers get the evaluations, training, standards, curriculum, assessments, and the student data to improve their practice." Gates is leaving out key ingredients that promote and cultivate learning in the classroom: commitment and accountability from students and parents, support from administrators, tools and resources (books, paper, technology) and enough teachers and counselors to support the students. To begin with, in poor areas of the city, where most of the failing schools in Philadelphia are located, huge numbers of high school students have very little accountability. The problems are so numerous, and the schools so underfunded, that at the end of the marking periods, teachers and administrators throw up their hands and let the students pass to the next level, then to the next grade. Did they master the material? No. With pressure on schools and principals to show graduation numbers, oftentimes, principals tell teachers to change grades, and to allow students to graduate. The unspoken message is often very clear: it is possible to graduate even if you put forth a minimal effort.

Teachers can tell you what is lacking in a lot of public schools. With poverty, comes stress, pain, hurt, and worry—all factors that can make it extremely challenging for a child to be open to learn. In the last few years, I have had students whose parents were in jail, several students who were shot during the school year due to neighborhood arguments and students who had just been released from jail themselves. One day in March at Vaux High School, Jerome's teacher noticed that after missing several days of school, he came to class and sat staring out the window, unresponsive. After class, she pulled him aside and asked him what was wrong. He disclosed to her that he had woke up one morning to find out that his mother had abandoned him and his young sister and had run off to live with her boyfriend. They were alone in the house with no food, and he was worried about how he was going to come up with the rent money. Many children barely make it to school each day because of the tough situations they are in. They need more than a great teacher.

In July 2012, President Obama announced his plan to create an elite corps of master teachers, a $1 billion program to increase U.S. students' achievement in science, technology, engineering, and math. The program that will reward high-performing teachers with salary stipends is part of a long-term effort by President Barack Obama to encourage education in high-demand areas that hold the key to future economic growth—and to close the achievement gap between American students and their international peers." Obama said his goal was to put a master teacher in every school. I have to ask, how is one master teacher going to help all of these children overwhelmed with poverty? How is this going to help someone like Jerome and his little sister?

Critics and reformers also propose better evaluations from administrators, more feedback and more professional development to enhance teaching. Teachers benefit from discussing with each other the issues that they have in the classrooms, and when schools give teachers a "common planning time," an hour in the day in which they can share strategies, ideas and discuss common students, it can be very productive. In another example of how non-educators are getting over-involved in our public education system, and misinforming the public, Steven Brill, founder of Court TV, advocate of corporate reform and author of *Class Warfare*, repeatedly referred to this hour in his book as a "free hour,"[57] as if teachers watch soap operas during any nonteaching time. The reality is that as teachers, we never stop working from the moment we walk in the school door. Any time outside of actual teaching is used for planning, correcting, tutoring, or collaborating with other teachers. During my lunch hour for example, I eat at my desk, administer make-up tests, or make photocopies and correct homework. Most teachers work well collaboratively, and want to improve their teaching, especially if it means improving our students' achievement.

In 2011 Duncan told educators at the National Board of Professional Teaching Standards Conference that teachers should have a starting salary of $60,000 and the opportunity to make up to $150,000. "Many bright people are attracted to teaching, but surveys say that they are reluctant to enter the field for the long haul. They see it as low-paying and low-prestige." [58] The lack of prestige comes from the public as well as from within the school system. If you read the comments from the public in our newspaper, *The Philadelphia Inquirer,* you will see that many people believe that teachers have it easy, they are lazy, and they complain too much. There is a lack of prestige within the system as well. Many principals in public schools do not demonstrate respect for the teachers' craft or opinions. Principals and vice-principals are paid from $90,000–$100,000 a year, while most teachers make anywhere from $40,000–$80,000 depending on years on the job and educational background. However, I have never heard complaints from teachers about their salaries. Instead, teachers discuss more immediate needs such as textbooks, support in the classroom, and more school police to help with violence.

Many reformers want to apply private sector principles to the teaching profession, and believe that by offering financial incentives, teachers will be inspired to work harder and increase student achievement. This idea implies that most teachers don't want their students to do well, and we need to be offered a bonus to change our goals. Teachers do not go into the field to make a lot of money. Most want to teach because they believe in the value of education and want to help young people. Bonuses or merit pay are not going to solve issues in the classroom, such as overcrowding, violence, or poverty. Many teachers would be happy to have those funds pay for teacher's aides, social services, or more Special Education teachers, because they know firsthand that solving these problems would have an immediate effect.

Washington DC has been discussing the concept of teacher incentives and merit pay in the last few years. In 2007, President Obama spoke out in support of teacher unions. Two years later, Obama expressed support of merit pay for teachers, a concept that the unions oppose. In a speech to the Hispanic Chamber of Commerce in 2009, he said, "Too many supporters of my party have resisted the idea of rewarding excellence in teaching with extra pay, even though we know it can make a difference in the classroom." [59] At the same time, Duncan called on the unions to look at things differently, and hinted that the administration was coming around to promoting teacher incentive pay. Duncan began to outline a plan to develop a new evaluation system for teachers, one that included student performance data tied to compensation. The administration is caught in the middle between unions that are against merit pay, and the influential and wealthy reformers who constantly promote it.

Since 2006, the federal government has promoted the Teacher Incentive Fund. This program was initiated by President George W. Bush's administration. The fund provides money to states and districts that utilize performance-pay programs for teachers in high needs schools. During the Bush administration, the program was never totally funded, and consequently got off to a slow start. On the U.S. Department of Education website, it explains, "This round of the (Teacher Incentive Fund) competition includes a new focus on supporting district-wide evaluation systems that reward success, offer greater professional opportunities, and drive decision-making on recruitment, development, and retention of effective teachers and principals."[60] The competition is based solely on applicants who "can implement and demonstrate plans for improving human capital in high-need schools through improved compensation systems that offer differentiated pay based on educator effectiveness, additional roles and responsibilities, and service in struggling schools."[61] The goals of the Teacher's Incentive Fund include "improving student achievement by increasing teacher and principal effectiveness, reforming teacher and principal compensation systems so that teachers and principals are rewarded for increases in student achievement, increasing the number of effective teachers, and sustainable performance-based compensation systems." Teachers often ask, "How are teachers going to improve schools and student test scores with little to no tools to do so?" Teachers need support for their students who struggle every day to read. If I am teaching a class of eleventh graders, and 40 percent of them cannot read above the sixth grade level, will I receive support for them? If not, how can I bring up test scores with such a wide disparity of skills in one classroom? Even though these incentive programs have been tried in the past with little success, the Department of Education continues to pursue these ideas.

In the 2007–2008 school year, New York City began its participation in a similar incentive program. It was a joint venture between the United Federation of Teachers and the New York City Department of Education. The program gave financial bonuses to high needs schools with improved performance. In a report published by CECR, the Center for Educator Compensation Reform, it states that the goals of the program were to:

- Provide incentives and rewards to teachers in high-need schools that successfully increase student achievement.
- Institute a revised system of professional compensation for teachers.
- Create a climate of collaboration among faculty members.[62]

The evaluations of the schools were based on standardized tests and progress towards graduation as well as graduation rates. If and when a school showed progress, it could receive up to $3,000 per full time UFT represented staff member. The principal and his committee would make the final decision about how much each person would receive. One hundred ninety-six schools participated in the program, and over $50 million dollars worth of bonuses were given over the three-year period. After three years, the program was analyzed by the Rand Corporation in partnership with Vanderbilt University and the National Center on Performance Incentives. They published a report in 2011 based on the three-year program.

The findings of the final report, published in 2011 were that there were no effects on student achievement at any grade level. Most eligible teachers earned a bonus of $3,000 for the year. Some teachers felt that after taxes, the bonus was not significant to inspire change, and that the eligibility was too focused on test scores. There was no reported change in motivation of the teachers. It is no surprise that most teachers are not motivated by money. Teachers want their students to succeed. But most teachers are more interested in getting the help that they need in the classroom, implementing tutoring programs, giving students individual attention, and being respected for their work, than receiving a bigger check.

The report of the NYC School Wide Performance Bonus Program also stated that the tests scores of the schools in the program were actually lower than schools outside of the program for all three years. Regarding a monetary bonus as an incentive to be a more effective educator, one teacher said, "The money had no impact on my work ethic or anything

I do. My kids working in my class that makes me happy. My kids being productive and excelling and learning and becoming good citizens that's important to me. If I were a money person, I don't think I would have gone into teaching to begin with."[63] Proponents of the program expected teachers to be more motivated by money to change their practices. But, during the program, the only thing that changed was the offering of bonuses. The teachers' working environments, the classrooms, and the student body did not. It reminds me of the first year I came to work at Vaux, in the first year of the Promise Academies in Philadelphia, one of our teachers, a twenty-three year veteran at the same school, commented, "Every year they come out with some new program. Watch-it will be gone in a couple of years. You can paint the building a new color, put up more artwork in the hallways, but it is still the same student body." She was right—two years after the Promise Academy model was initiated, the lack of funding caused so many cuts in the program, that there is very little evidence of improvements in these schools.

In June 2009, Race to the Top (RTT) was announced as a government initiative and $4.35 billion dollar contest to inspire innovation and change in our school systems across the country. States can apply to the federal government for funding based on selection criteria worth 500 points. The different criteria are based on increasing teacher effectiveness, state reform, standards, and assessment, improving failing schools and data systems. President Obama seems to be genuinely behind the teachers of our country, but I am not sure he truly understands what we need to make a difference. In his speech to the Urban League, he stated, "I want teachers to have better salaries, I want them to have more support, I want them to be trained like the professionals that they are— with rigorous residencies like the ones doctors go though. I want them to have a fulfilling and supportive workplace environment. I want them to have the resources—from basic supplies to reasonable class sizes-that help them to succeed."[64] These statements show an understanding of the things educators are lacking. Then why has RTT been so narrowly focused on teacher evaluation systems and data?

It is 2012, and the Department of Education is still pursuing teacher incentive programs, even after the evidence from New York City Schools showed no relationship between bonus or incentives and student performance. The government continues to support the concept of merit pay through the Teacher Incentive Fund and the Race to the Top program. Race to the Top rewards funding to states who can demonstrate a commitment to improving student outcomes in many ways including, "compensating, promoting, and retaining teachers and principals, including by providing opportunities for highly effective teachers and principals (both as defined in this notice) to obtain additional compensation and be given additional responsibilities."[65] Critics of RTT also insist that by focusing even more on test scores, there is a greater chance of testing fraud, which has happened in several cities already, including Atlanta, Philadelphia, and New York City. With budget cuts wiping out entire budgets in many school districts, teachers and staff are receiving lay off notices and student programs are being eliminated. School districts are desperate for more money.

One of the problems with RTT is that in order to prove effectiveness, there is a dependence on data. In fact, one of the criteria for the grant is creating and implementing data systems to support instruction, and demonstrating the use of data to improve it. Having access to data means testing, and insuring that students do well on tests often means hours and hours of test preparation, which is still one of the main criticisms of No Child Left Behind. "States would be rewarded for having policies authorizing aggressive interventions for failing schools. They'd be significantly penalized for lacking a charter school law. And they'd be barred from even applying if they had "data firewalls" preventing student performance information from being tied to individual teachers. States also earned significant points for crafting plans that earned the blessing of their school districts and unions.[66] In an interview with Jon Stewart, Duncan explained that RTT wants to tap into the resources of the local talent of each school district, allowing the local teachers and administrators to come up with their own programs.

However, the fact that their programs must follow specific guidelines set by the Department of Education means that opportunity to innovate is limited. RTT is a competition for districts that need to apply for the grants and demonstrate their plan to implement change.[67] Union buy-in is extremely difficult because most teachers are opposed to student test scores tied to teacher evaluations.

Another criticism of RTT is that districts must propose reforms that haven't been tested for effectiveness. The process is so hurried that there is no time to evaluate results and the strengths of the programs. Others believe that the program is too focused on teacher evaluations and the promotion of charter schools. To be eligible for RTT funds, some states must agree to change laws that prohibit using test scores to evaluate teachers. Many critics have complained that these formulas are not backed up with evidence, so we are adopting strategies that have no basis in fact.

In the end, the study of NYC schools showed "no statistically significant relationship between student achievement and bonus award plans."[68] The program was abandoned in 2010. Perhaps increasing teacher salaries across the board would attract more teachers. There are many talented professionals, either working in other fields, or in college, who would like to teach in public schools, and are reluctant because of the low pay. But to just offer incentives and bonuses to existing teachers has so far proven to be ineffective.

Every year, I have seen many great teachers discouraged and worn down by the working conditions and lack of respect from the principal that they express a desire to give up teaching altogether. Low morale means teachers are less inspired and less energetic to go the extra mile. By March of the last school year, the low morale in my high school in Philadelphia was apparent in the teachers' faces when you walked down the hall. It came from many factors, but it was not about a low salary. It came from unfair treatment, not being treated as professionals, and high incidents of violence in the classroom with very little understanding and support from the administration. Blatant disregard for our safety, working conditions and the learning environment in which students are expected to excel is common in our public schools. This lack of understanding and compassion for what teachers do on a daily basis on the part of a principal is exactly what negatively affects a teacher's performance and effort in the classroom. We are disrespected and cursed at every day by the students. Teachers deserve more from the leader of the school.

Teachers would like to be recognized as professionals. At our high school last year, our principal did not once thank the teachers. Most of us work an average of twenty unpaid hours a week. The fact that she didn't acknowledge the teachers' hard work made a huge impression on many of us. Teachers would like to be appreciated by the administration, not necessarily with money, but an acknowledgement would make a huge difference. On the last day of school this year, our principal gave out certificates to her staff, and a handful of teachers who worked on special committees, but did not acknowledge our efforts as a group. However, she did take a moment to say to us, "Teaching is not for all of you." She then announced all of the teachers who were leaving the school. Twenty out of sixty teachers had decided to move on from the school or quit teaching altogether. What does this say about the working environment?

The problem with this attitude is that teachers are treated as if they are disposable commodities. The teacher didn't work out? Let them go, push them to another school, let some other principal deal with them. This is the way that many feel about merit pay programs, that they are designed to weed out teachers without looking at the big picture- all the elements that affect a student's performance. If we tie a teacher's salary to students' test results, we are equating them with salespeople, rewarding them for numbers of high scores, like a car salesman who gets bonuses for selling a lot of cars. Neither teachers, nor students should be evaluated this way. We cannot blindly apply business principles to the field of education. Public education is complicated, because the most influential factors that affect successes are so difficult to measure: family involvement, financial status, and personal motivation, to name a few.

Chapter Six

PUBLIC SCHOOL REFORM AND BIG MONEY

There is money to be made in the privatization of schools. Special interest groups who see money-making opportunities in the field of education are at the forefront of the reform movement today. According to the *Huffington Post*, "The K-12 market is tantalizingly huge: The United States spends more than $500 billion a year to educate kids from ages five to eighteen."[69] In the past, aside from textbook and test prep companies, it was difficult for private companies to break into the business of education. Today, it seems to be an opportune time for big businesses to jump in, and many are discussing endless possibilities to make money in American education, from charter schools to cyber schools. The problem is, many of these investors are savvy business people, but have no background in education; thus, they are in a rush to make profit, but do not invest time in researching what is needed to create successful schools. With NCLB came the chance to "turnaround" underperforming schools into privately operated charter schools. Today, investors are discussing using technology to write and grade tests, and even to replace teachers in the classrooms with online teachers to cut down on labor costs.

In the last ten years, millions of dollars have been invested nationally into researching ways to change our public school system. Today, the push from corporate reformers (mostly made up of wealthy self-interest groups looking for investments) is to convert public schools into privately run charter schools, and to push children into cyber schools. Diane Ravitch recently claimed, "This is a new frontier. The private equity guys and the hedge fund guys are circling public education."[70] Of the 5,500 charter schools around the country, many are run by private companies who want to cut costs and increase profit, but at what sacrifice to the quality of education? The goals of corporate reformers include making public education accessible to private investment, and turning public education into a marketplace in which parents and students are consumers of a product—an education. Reformers today believe that if there were more competition within the field of education, schools would rise to the challenge, and outcomes would improve.

Gates has been very involved in educational reform for over ten years, through his philanthropic organization, the Bill and Melinda Gates Foundation. Gates' reform policies have focused largely on issues such as the teacher seniority system and the use of student test scores to rate teachers. Gates' power and influence cannot be overlooked. Some even worry that the size of his influence and financial investments is so large that it might "squelch independent thought."[71] He has contributed to colleges and universities, such as Harvard, which has received $3.5 million, to support and implement his ideas. According to the New York Times, "The foundation spent $373 million on education in 2009, the latest year for which its tax returns are available, and devoted $78 million to advocacy—quadruple the amount spent on advocacy in 2005. Over the next five or six years, … the foundation expects to pour $3.5 billion more into education, up to 15 percent of it on advocacy."[72] Public school teachers often question how a billionaire who attended the most prestigious high school in Seattle could possibly understand the challenges of our public school system. In fact, his comments about what students and teachers need often angers many educators.

When Gates first got involved with education, it was through the small schools initiative, a plan to redesign the traditional large high school model into smaller schools. Today, one of his big pushes is to overhaul the way teachers are evaluated, which continues to be controversial. The New Teacher Project, financed by Gates, has studied teacher evaluation systems, and influenced decision making in Washington, DC. He contributed $2 million dollars to the movie, *Waiting for Superman*, which promoted the concept of charter schools, and contributed $4 million dollars to help to extend mayoral control over public schools in New York City. Gates and other wealthy reformists prefer mayoral control of a school system because it allows them to more easily influence the schools, by only having to convince the mayor of their agenda, instead of an entire public school board. A mayor can push an idea through the system quicker, with less worry about opposition. In 2009, Gates donated $4 million of his own money to Learn NY, an organization that led public relations campaigns and lobbying in Albany to overturn a law that limits mayoral terms, in order to allow Bloomberg to run for a third term. The mayor ran on a platform that pushed his education agenda.

Today in New York City, as charter schools are opening up in place of failing schools, many large schools have been converted into smaller schools. This has caused problems when several schools have been forced to share one building; losing precious space for libraries and needed classrooms. Many new charters have pushed out existing public schools, causing the public schools to give up classrooms and cram large classes that often hold Special Education students and English language learners into overcrowded spaces. Ten years and billions of dollars spent, yet many public schools are still operating on shoestring budgets. Poor high schools students have graduated unprepared for the workforce, and 40 percent of the children in my classes at Vaux were not provided with special services they were entitled to, are now nineteen and sadly undereducated. They have been passed on and forgotten.

Gates and his team of reformists have been hugely influential in our nation's capital. *The Washington Post* reported in 2010 that many of former Gates officials now work under our U.S. Secretary of Education, Arne Duncan, "including Jim Shelton, former education program director at the foundation and now Assistant Deputy Secretary for "Innovation and Improvement." Joanne Weiss has already been promoted from heading its "Race to the Top" fund to become Duncan's chief of staff.[73] Gates' ideas and agendas have now infiltrated Washington policymaking. Weiss was formerly chief operating officer of the New Schools Venture Fund, which finances charter school expansion with dollars provided by Gates. The new Gates reform pushes ideas such as new teacher evaluation systems, getting rid of unions that protect teachers' rights, and the replacement of neighborhood public schools with charter schools. Some see this as Gates' agenda to control and influence our public school system through his millions. Many of his ideas for reform have been supported by Duncan, and are now being translated into federal programs such as "Race To The Top," which makes funds available to empty-handed states as long as they follow the agenda of the corporate reformers: abolish seniority, fire existing teachers, get rid of the unions, tie student test scores to teacher evaluations, and replace failing schools with privately run charter schools.

Another idea that has repeatedly surfaced is the concept of vouchers. Opponents see the controversial vouchers as another dangerous way of redirecting public funds to private schools. As proposed, most programs across the country would distribute monetary vouchers (usually with a value of $2,500-$5,000, based on the amount the system would spend per student) to parents of school-age children, mostly in inner-city schools. Parents could then use the vouchers to pay for tuition at private and parochial schools. It has been tried in several states around the country, with limited success. For example, in 2004 Congress came up with a plan to give 1,700 students in Washington, DC a voucher of up to $7,500 to attend private and religious schools in the city as alternatives to public schools. However, in 2009, under intense pressure from the teachers unions, Congress and the Administration began to dismantle the program and no new students are participating today. Many states have voted down these proposals, and now the new push for privatization continues under the name of "choice," through the promotion of charter and cyber schools.

There is big money to be made in the ideas that are proposed by corporate reformers. If the millions of dollars that Gates has spent in the last ten years to "experiment" with reform ideas had been invested in our public schools, our inner city schools might have seen improvement by now. Why are so many wealthy businesspersons becoming involved in the field of education? Are they genuinely interested in making the lives of our poor students better? Do they see potential in poor inner-city children? Have they come to the inner-city classrooms to see what really goes on, to see what the real issues that impede progress for these children?

Ravenel Boykin Curry IV went to Yale and Harvard Business School. Today, he manages hedge funds and works for Eagle Capital Management, a company founded by his father. After a meeting in 1991 with a group of superintendents, he became interested in investing in education, and soon after became involved in the formation of Girl's Prep, a charter school in Manhattan, which opened in 2004. According to Steven Brill, "his interest in education reform was serious and sophisticated. He was not just chasing a fad."[74] Curry explains why he got involved in educational reform, "People like us—long term investors—like education reform," Curry explains, because first, we are typically geeks who care about numbers, and we can see that the numbers in education just don't add up: more and more money but no better results. Second, it's easy to see that education is a great investment of what you invest in really changes things. It's classic leverage. A relatively small amount of money produces better lives and people who can support our economy instead of having to get handouts from it …Third, it's classic long-term investing, which is what all of us do. Fourth, it's something where we think we can add value, because we can help create business plans for charters …Fifth, it's exciting and fun for people like us, who usually only work with numbers, to work on something like this. We're nerds who don't get to do exciting stuff in our day jobs. And sixth, because so many of us got interested in this at the same time, you get to work with people who are your friends."[75] Curry has many reasons that he got into the business of educational reform, most of them are based on self-interest, not on helping children.

What are the goals of corporate reformers? Under the designation of "choice," they want to privatize our public schools, making the neighborhood schools last resort institutions, where poor children who cannot choose will end up. So many of my students in the last few years would not be able to choose a school because of their family situations. They would remain in the neighborhood schools, which as funds are diverted to charters and cyber schools, would remain underfunded and without needed resources. Jerome, whose mother abandoned him and his little sister to run away with her boyfriend could not access an online school. Tyreek whose mother thinks a "D" is good enough would most likely think that a neighborhood school is "good enough," and Robert, who is MMR would not be able to use an online school, and would most likely not get into a charter school.

Corporate reformers also want to use unreliable test scores to evaluate teachers, ignoring all of the elements that affect test scores, such as hunger, social promotion, mental health issues, drug addiction, and teen pregnancy, to name just a few of the roadblocks to learning for our poor children.

In 1999, William Bennett, former Secretary of Education under Ronald Reagan, Michael Milken, (most famous for being indicted on ninety-eight counts of racketeering and securities fraud in 1989 as the result of an insider trading investigation), and Ronald J. Packard, (formerly of McKinsey & Company and Goldman Sachs) founded K12 Inc, the for-profit online school whose mission, according to its website is "To provide any child access to exceptional curriculum and tools that enable him or her to maximize his or her success in life, regardless of geographic, financial, or demographic circumstance."76 The business of cyber schools is growing. K12, the biggest online school in the country, expected a profit of $72 million in 2011. They spent $26.5 million on advertising in 2010, and if you live in Pennsylvania, you can see the TV ads and billboards all over the city. They push hard to recruit new students, and the school pays sign up bonuses to employees for recruiting new clients. Unfortunately, the results have not been all that favorable. According to an analysis by the *New York Times*, "Nearly 60 percent of its students are behind grade level in math. Nearly 50 percent trail in reading. A third do not graduate on time. And hundreds of children, from kindergartners to seniors, withdraw within months after they enroll." But the company, which went public in 2007, is thriving, reporting a 35 percent jump in earnings in the third quarter of 2011 to 130 million.77

Promoted as an alternative to the traditional "brick and mortar" school and for children who do not work well in the public school classroom, K12 is profiting from the instability of our public schools. Children stay at home, communicate with teachers through the Internet, get assignments, and work online. On the K12 website, it advises parents that they must be prepared to help their kids for several hours a day. In order to be successful in this kind of learning environment, a student needs to be very self-motivated. This is a huge problem for inner-city students, who even in high school, need to be supervised and encouraged throughout most classes. While I can think of a handful of students who would benefit from online schools, I think it is dangerous to assume it is an end-all solution for huge numbers of children.

Two years ago, I taught Angela for two hours a day. She was very bright and independently motivated. Unfortunately, she also had been diagnosed with Oppositional Defiant Disorder, which is characterized by tendencies to argue with adults, having few or no friends, being in constant trouble at school, being easily annoyed, spiteful, and having a bad temper. Angela would have great moments of brilliance. When she paid attention, she usually got the right answer, raising her hand first to answer the question. She was capable of making all "As" in her classes. But unfortunately she was in a constant battle with her teachers and classmates. One day she would get along with everyone, and then the next day she would walk over to someone and pull their hair or throw a notebook at them. In her English class, she threw a garbage can across the room when asked to step outside. After repeatedly being asked to come for a conference with the principal or her teachers, her mother removed her and enrolled her in a cyber school. She would probably be a good candidate for this type of school because she worked better on her own, and was self-motivated. But if K12 were only marketing to this type of student, they would not be making the same profits they do today. The advantage that Angela had though was a mother who spoke up for her daughter, researched schools, and options. So many parents living in poverty don't have the resources, or the motivation to do so. However, K12 proposes to be a great option for all students.

On their website, K12 states that their mission "has remained steadfast: To provide *any* child access to exceptional curriculum and tools that enable him or her to maximize his or her success in life, regardless of geographic, financial, or demographic circumstance. They go on to say that "K12 offers outstanding, highly effective curriculum that enables mastery of core concepts and skills for *all kinds of minds.*"[78] I challenge them that an online school can work for all kinds of students. This would not work for the student who wants to be class president, because this type of student needs social interaction, discussion, and debate. This would not work for the child who is behind in math and science, and needs to have one-on-one tutoring. This would not work for students like Shanice, who told me last year, "When you explain it to me by myself, I get it." It would not work for 80 percent of the students at my public high school in Philadelphia, who don't have Internet at home (at an inner-city school, I cannot assign research homework because most kids cannot get online once they leave school).

In addition, as the website states, parents must be involved, which presents several problems. K12 states that, "Parents of children in grades

K-6 can expect to spend three to five hours per day supporting their child's education."[79] This is a major commitment for many parents. Even though I wholly support the idea of parents helping their children with their education, is this realistic to expect that all parents can do this? In addition, many of the parents of my students were struggling students themselves, and are not equipped to tutor their children in many of the subjects.

English language learners are excluded from this option, because many of their parents, who do not read or write in English, would not be able to help. What about the Special Education student who lives in poverty and does not have Internet at home? This student (of which 30 percent of my students were this year) is already struggling in a public school because he needs individualized attention, would not benefit from a cyber school. How many students are self-motivated enough to manage their own school schedules, read, study, and learn all alone, manage to utilize the online teachers as resources and achieve satisfactory grades with little guidance? The problem with the cyber school concept is it has been created to make a profit. To make a profit, you need consistent enrollment. K12 pushes the concept on parents and all students, without carefully considering if this is an appropriate option for each individual. I cannot think of more than a handful of my students in the past five years who would be capable of handling this kind of independent study. But then I teach poor inner-city kids.

Yet, as many wealthy entrepreneurs have found out in the past ten years, kids equal money. So they push to get kids enrolled, and figure out whether it is a good fit for the child later. Because of the growing possibilities for financial gain, there is a dangerous sense of urgency to capitalize on and profit from children and education. In northern Colorado, COVA (Colorado Virtual Academy), which is managed by K12 reported an enrollment of 5,000 in 2011. Last year, in the Adams 12 Five Star School District north of Denver, when the district was discovering it had a $25 million dollar deficit and was discussing laying off 155 employees, K12 was projecting an annual growth of $100 million dollars.[80]

K12 is funded almost exclusively by public dollars. The company receives around $5,500-$6,000 from state government for each enrolled student, which means that neighborhood schools lose this money. When we look closer at K12, we find out that there is a huge dropout and turnover rate. Parents enroll their child; they might last a few months, and then withdraw. Pennsylvania's Agora School (run by K12) reported that 2,6888 students dropped out in the 2009-2010 school year. Parents enroll their child, the school collects the money, and then several months later, the child drops out.

In Colorado, the state spends $5,900 for each student and many are asking, "Who are these online schools accountable to?" Schools are running on slashed budgets, yet K12 is recording huge profits. In Colorado, COVA teachers have complained that there were students on their class lists who never once logged in, which means that the company collected (public) money for them, but the students never attended a single class. K12 collects taxpayers' money to run their schools, and in Pennsylvania, about 30,000 students are enrolled in online schools at a cost of about $10,000 per student. According to the state auditor general, this doubles or more what it takes to educate the students online. "It is extremely unfair for a taxpayer to be paying for extra expenses, such as advertising."[81] There is great money to be made, and it appears to be a great scam.

Ronald J. Packard stated, "Kids have been shackled to their brick and mortar school down the block for too long. He also has stated that "75 percent of those kids coming in are behind more than one grade level," which as a teacher who has worked with children who are behind several years, I have to question whether sitting them in front of a computer and expecting them to teach themselves is a sound decision. But, in a business, the profits make the decision. According to the *New York Times*, "Because many states prohibit for-profit public education, the management companies for virtual schools run schools under contract with public districts or nonprofit charter schools, which also receive public money. But companies like K12 are almost fully in charge—devising curriculum, hiring teachers and principals and evaluating student performance."[82]

With little supervision, students are getting away with doing little work. Moreover, with the large numbers of students dropping out, K12 teachers have felt pressured to pass kids who do not complete their assignments. If many of these students are those who are behind a year, it is most likely because they have learning difficulties, which could be attributed to many factors—home issues, poverty, attention deficit problems, behavioral problems, or the inability to focus. How is an online school going to address these issues? Putting the child in front of a computer at home with little supervision, and distractions of cell phones and television would make it extremely difficult to be productive. Children who have difficulties in the classroom will not necessarily do better outside of the classroom. In fact, for many students, what is missing is one-on-one help, something that public schools do not have money to fund, and cyber schools do not provide.

In the 1970s, a New England educator named Ray Budde came up with the idea that small groups of teachers be given contracts or "charters" to explore new alternatives to public schools. He presented the concept in a paper he entitled, "Education by Charter," published in 1974. The idea slowly caught on across the country, and in the late 1980s, Philadelphia started a number of schools-within-schools and called them "charters." The idea that came from Budde was to find a way for teachers to create autonomous schools that would be an alternative to the public schools. In December of 2011, The National Alliance for Public Charter Schools (NAPCS) announced that the number of students attending public charter schools across the country was more than two million, and that over 500 new public charter schools opened their doors in the 2011–12 school year.[83]

Proponents of charter schools believe that charters provide parents with a choice for their children, and that choice, which had been nonexistent in public education for many years, translates into a healthy competition and drives up the quality of schools. Charter schools are public schools and like district public schools, they are funded according to enrollment, and receive money from the district and the state according to the number of students attending. However, many charter schools receive private funding, and are able to pay their CEOs hefty salaries, and provide extra services that public schools cannot (public schools do not receive private money to pay principals and staff). When Eva Moskowitz, who today runs Success Academy Charter Schools in New York City, was being courted in 2005 to run a new network of New York charter schools, the financial model was explained as follows: "Charter schools got the same money per pupil from the state and city to cover costs as public schools did ...other support costs—such as the salary of the CEO to run the network, extra training, financial and operations staffing, and recruiting new students and planning new schools—would be financed by the network's umbrella (private) organization."[84] Charter schools often have a lot more money to work with.

Proponents of charter schools believe that public schools will improve their programs with such competition. However, it is difficult to say how this could happen when so many public schools are constantly reporting budget cuts, and can barely hold onto teachers, let alone create new programs. How can public schools compete with no funds to work with?

The first charter appeared in NYC in 1999, and today in NYC, the number has grown to 136. Reports have surfaced about the unfavorable working conditions at certain charter schools. In fact, according to a report published by the New York Center for Charter Schools, about a third of teachers leave charter schools each year, (the rate for public district schools is closer to 15 percent), due to the unreasonable workload. As stated in the report, "The report finds that charter schools, on average, have higher rates of teacher and principal turnover compared to NYC district schools. Such rates of turnover are, in part, consistent with a dynamic, growing and still quite new sector, and one which operates with different background labor rules and more varied compensation structures….." "Charter school leaders are paying close attention to this issue, and seeking ways to improve educator pipelines and keep effective educators on the job longer."[85]

According to a report published in June 2012 by the U.S. Government Accountability Office, charter schools are not doing a good job of addressing the needs of Special Education students. Some people report that charter schools discourage parents of SPED students, and "counsel out" many students who do not do well in their school, which in the end could negatively affect the numbers of successful students. This is something that public schools are unable to do. In 2008, in New York City, one student named Mathew Sprowal was selected by a lottery to go to Harlem Success Academy 3 Charter School. His mother was excited about his future at the school. Mathew's experience did not turn out as he expected, when he was "distracted and disruptive" in class. After only a few weeks at the school, Mathew's mother received an e-mail from the school, questioning whether Mathew was a good fit for the school. The next week, after evaluating him, the school psychologist told his mother that he would probably be happier elsewhere, and she was encouraged to send him back to a public school. Mathew enrolled in his neighborhood public school, leaving the charter experience behind him. He was later diagnosed with an attention deficit disorder, but he is doing well in his public school today.[86] Charter schools cannot afford to have students who cannot produce good numbers, and Special Education students mean lower scores. It is easier to encourage them to find other schools than to try to educate them. I spent two months in a charter school in Philadelphia. One of the teachers in a meeting made the one comment that will always stay in my mind. We were discussing students with behavior problems and he said, "We have go to get rid of these bad kids before they ruin our numbers."

The pressure is on to show that charter schools work, and many of them cannot afford to risk their numbers by allowing disruptive students or students with special needs in their schools. This has been an ongoing criticism of charter schools. Even though the reports of success have been mixed, (most agree that there are good and bad charter schools), charter schools can control their student body. This makes it unfair to compare charters with public schools, who must admit all students, whether they just came from a disciplinary school, have IEPs, behavioral problems, read five years below their grade level, or they just got out of jail.

Proponents of charter schools claim that in public schools, teachers do not teach, but that in charter schools, great teaching goes on every day. In *Class Warfare,* Steven Brill tells the story about the Harlem Success Academy I, where he spent time researching for his book. It is housed in the same building as a traditional public school, and it was easy to move back and forth between the two schools to compare them. Just as in the movie, *Waiting For Superman*, critics of public schools love to tell stories of public school teachers who are so incompetent that they sit all day with their feet up on the desk, barking orders at the students. Of course, down the hall in the charter school, as he tells it, one young teacher worked tirelessly, never stopping and never sitting down. Insulting public school teachers makes for exciting journalism. Brill is a businessman and journalist, not a teacher. I have taught in five schools, have worked in seven public schools, and I have never once seen a teacher with their feet on their desk. At the end of his book, Brill reveals that this brilliant young charter schoolteacher decided to quit because the workload was too much for her. Welcome to the American Public Education System; we work long hours and we rarely sit down.

It is difficult to compare charters with neighborhood public schools, who must admit all neighborhood kids who walk in the door. A recent analysis of the Harlem Village Academy, a charter school that was featured in the movie *Waiting for Superman*, demonstrates a similar problem of student populations that do not reflect their public school counterparts. This frustrates public school advocates because they feel that charter schools are not represented honestly, and are promoted as a better, more successful option to public schools. Of course, a school will be more successful if they can pick and choose their students. In the report published by the U.S. Government Accountability Office, it states that 11 percent of students enrolled in public schools during the 2009-2010 school year had disabilities, compared with 8 percent of students in charter schools. This has not been my experience in the last two years, when I taught in two different failing schools in inner city Philadelphia, where I had anywhere from 30 to 50 percent Special Education students in my classes. In both of these schools, the population was anywhere from 92 to 98 percent African American, with a small number of English Language Learners (ELLs).

In many public schools today, the number of students who are not proficient in English is much larger, and critics of charters say that they are not admitting as many ELL students either. According to an article in *The Notebook*, "three fourths of the school system's English language learners are found at nine high schools in Philadelphia, most of them among the city's most dangerous and poorest performing. In 2007–2008, 1,675 of the 2,270 ELLs were in district high schools that were in "Corrective Action II" status; in other words, they had not made "Annual Yearly Progress" for at least five years.[87] The concentration of ELL students in troubled urban schools is a national trend that helps explain their relatively low achievement, researchers say. "This new pattern of segregation tends not to be just of color, but also about poverty and linguistic isolation," said a study released this summer by the Center for Immigration Studies at New York University and the Pew Hispanic Center.[88] Critics of charter schools say that charters fail to admit many ELL students, and they are often left in schools that are underfunded.

The cost of public education in the United States is estimated to cost over $500 billion a year. Private money, coming from wealthy philanthropists has influenced public policy all over the country, especially in Washington, DC. Along with Gates, two other influential foundations include the Eli and Edythe Broad Foundation and the Walton Family Foundation, which have spent hundreds of millions of dollars on school reform. All three support the same concepts of reform: high-stakes testing used to weed out bad teachers through new teacher evaluation systems, and charter and cyber schools to replace public schools.

Parents, eager to find an alternative for their children have enrolled them in charter schools, with mixed results. In 2009, Stanford University released a report on charter schools, and stated, "17 percent of charter schools reported academic gains that were significantly better than traditional public schools, while 37 percent of charter schools showed gains that were worse than their traditional public school counterparts, with 46 percent of charter schools demonstrating no significant difference."[89]

In *Waiting For Superman*, a documentary that was released in 2010, the message of the film supported the corporate reform agenda: (1) public schools are failing, and the reason is that public school teachers are of low quality; (2) public schools spend so much money already that more money will not help the problem; and (3) charter schools, funded by public money, but run by private companies are the answer to educating the poor children. The movie was written and directed by Davis Guggenheim, of an *Inconvenient Truth*, who did not attend public school, but instead went to the Sidwell Friends School, a private school where his children attend today. One of the central messages of the film is that public schools have bad teachers, and that our government should get rid of the evil unions that protect bad teachers and keep them in the classrooms. The film did not address this question however: if teachers from private, public, and suburban schools all graduate from the same universities and colleges, how could public school teachers be "less qualified"? Could it possibly be due to the lack of resources available to them? Could it be that the students that attend public schools have a lower socioeconomic status, and this affects their performance? Private schools do not pay their teachers more (in fact, most private schools pay teachers less), so it is not likely the teacher salaries that make the difference. Somehow, though, Guggenheim wants us to believe that it must be the fault of the teachers and the public school systems. If only we could turn all the failing schools into charters, he proposes.

Ignoring the effects of poverty on a child's ability to learn, Guggenheim suggests that public schools already spend millions of dollars, so it cannot be the money. He presents statistics that demonstrate an increase in spending per pupil over the last few decades. He visits one public school in Harlem to point out the dismal environment in which these children are educated. However, the director does not look at what poverty does to a child's ability to reason, focus, and concentrate. Instead he says, "Poor conditions of life do not lead to poor education, but it is a poor education which leads to poor conditions of life."[90] This seems to be the mantra of the corporate reformers today. Even President Obama and Secretary of Education Duncan suggest that children need an education to get out of poverty, that poverty should not get in the way of getting an education. In my experience, it does. Just ask Tiffany, whose mother is in jail, and finds it hard to motivate herself to come to school. She missed over forty days while in my class. Or ask Semajah, who does not live with her mom anymore because she is an addict, and now lives with a foster mother. She missed around twenty-three days of school spring quarter. Or you can ask Lashai, who at sixteen has two kids, and just got out of jail. She missed around three months of school this year. Dan Conway said it best when he wrote, "One can't help but note the irony of a documentary about education which sets out to systematically miseducate its audience about the nature of current social and political reality."[91]

Two of the schools that were featured in the film as success stories were the Harlem Children's Zone in NYC, and the KIPP schools, which operate in twenty states today.

The Harlem Children's Zone's president and chief executive officer is Geoffrey Canada, who has been with the school for over twenty years, and is now nationally recognized for his work in educational reform. In 1997, the school was launched as the Harlem Children's Zone Project in central Harlem. The Zone Project today covers 100 blocks and has an enrollment of close to 900 students from grades one to twelve. It serves a local community, and of its student body, 88 percent receive free lunch, 90 percent are Black, 1 percent White, 8 percent Hispanic, and 0 percent Asian. Admission to the school is based on a lottery, as demonstrated in the movie to be heartwrenching for the students who try, but do not get in.

On its website, it states that the Zone Project combines educational, social, and medical services. Some of the social services that it offers include: "Single Stop (offering services such as public benefits, access to legal guidance, financial advice, debt relief counseling and domestic crisis resolution); The Asthma Initiative (working closely with asthmatic children and their families so they can learn to manage the disease and lessen its effects); The Obesity Initiative (a multipronged program designed to help children and their families reverse the alarming trend toward obesity and its corresponding health problems in the community); The Family Development Program, (specializes in access to mental health professionals who collaborate with caseworkers to support therapeutic interventions); The Family Support Center (specializes in providing crisis intervention services, referrals, advocacy, groups on parenting and anger management training); Project Class (specializes in providing referrals to drug and alcohol abuse programs, as well as creating, implementing and monitoring drug treatment service plans. It recently added the Babies Initiative, which is offered to twenty families with children ages five and under who are at immediate risk of being put in foster care) and Truancy Prevention (specializes in providing referrals to drug and alcohol abuse programs, as well as creating, implementing and monitoring drug treatment service plans. It recently added the Babies Initiative, which is offered to twenty families with children ages five and under who are at immediate risk of being put in foster care.)"[92]

As a public school teacher reading about these programs, I am envious. I am familiar with the needs of my students and know that if public schools could offer these services, it would make a huge difference every day. Harlem Children's Zone has the luxury of receiving huge private donations, which public schools do not.

In a report by *Forbes* magazine, HCZ was on the list of the 200 largest charities. In the fiscal year of 2010, HCZ had reported total revenue of $69 million dollars, $10 million of which came from the government and $66 million that was donated privately. *Forbes* also reported Canada's yearly income as $450,872.

Waiting for Superman was successful in getting the message out to the public, and to motivate huge donations to the cause. Oprah Winfrey, who promoted the movie on her show, announced that she would donate $6 million dollars to six charter school organizations. Charter School Growth Fund, a Denver venture capitalist company, announced that it had secured $100 million dollars for charter schools from various sources such as the Walton Foundation. On the East Coast, Mark Zuckerberg, founder of Facebook, announced his $100 million donation to the state of New Jersey, to support Governor Chris Christie and Newark Mayor Cory Booker's new initiatives, including making it easier to get rid of ineffective teachers and doing away with tenure. On August 7, 2012, Governor Christie signed a new law, under which teachers and administrators could lose their tenure if they have two consecutive years of ineffective ratings. Christie supports the new reformer's agenda of blaming teachers for our educational system's inadequacy. On the state website, it states, "Governor Christie's Reform Agenda turns the current system inside out and finally puts effective, quality teaching ahead of seniority and lackluster results. This includes getting rid of the old salary system, which gave teachers the ability to make more money if they had higher degrees and more years on the job. Christie agrees with Gates that experience in the classroom doesn't matter. He also proposes on his website that he will push for more parental involvement through "empowering parents with access to quality data and additional outreach efforts."[93] On the website, it explains that "Governor Christie's Reform Agenda will increase parental involvement through parent-focused tools such as a help-desk, website, mailings, and forums. I suggest that the governor first poll the parents to see who in fact has access to the Internet. If the numbers are small, as they are in Philadelphia's public schools (five minutes across the Delaware River), this will not make much of a difference.

The three most powerful and influential contributors to educational reform today are the Gates Foundation, the Eli and Edythe Broad Foundation, and the Walton Family Foundation. All three have invested millions of dollars to influence and control public school reform in the past decade. The Broad Foundation has invested money into the training of successful professionals to serve in the field of education. The concept is that if someone has been successful in a government, corporate or military career, they could use those talents to turn around our education system. The Broad Superintendents Academy pays for the travel and tuition for its candidates to participate in six extended weekend classes that will prepare them to be superintendents. These executives have no background in education, have never been teachers, and most likely have not set foot into public school classrooms. In the academy, they are trained on all of the Broad Foundation agendas, and then they are hired by school districts around the country to implement the Broad Foundation ideals. In 2009, 43 percent of all large urban superintendent positions were filled by the Broad Academy graduates. Another initiative, the Broad Residency program, puts professionals with master's degrees into managerial positions in public school districts, charter schools and government positions. Broad subsidizes 50 percent of their salaries the first year and 25 percent the second year to get them started.[94] The problem is that many of these people have never been teachers, and are far removed from the classroom. Teachers prefer administrators and people in managerial positions in schools to have classroom experience to understand better the needs of teachers and students.

But the one foundation that has exercised the most power over educational reform, is the Gates Foundation, whose leverage pervades our government and decision making at the federal level. Even though study after study supports the idea that poverty plays a huge part in the roadblock to success for many students, these reformers choose to continue to ignore it. Instead, these wealthy and hugely influential foundations have come up with their own philosophies about what is needed in our American schools, and they have the money to put their theories into practice.

Since Gates first got interested the field of educational reform over ten years ago, he has spent millions of dollars in experimentation with our schools and children. In the beginning of his venture into education, he was convinced that if only we divided large schools into many smaller schools, student achievement would rise. Unfortunately, in the schools where Gates set up his small schools initiatives, results were dismal. "It's been a decade of learning," Gates said in an interview in 2011.[95] (Meanwhile, thousands of children in poverty have graduated from failing schools with little to show for it because of the lack of funding for the services they need). Once the Gates Foundation realized that this formula was not bringing results, they changed tack. In 2008, Gates announced that they were re-focusing their efforts on teachers. They admitted that the small schools project did not produce the expected results, and at that point were going to begin a new push for performance-based teacher pay, turning schools around, focusing on national standards and data collecting. One of Gates' early successful forays into public policy was *The Turnaround Challenge,* a "how-to" guide to turning around schools, in which the Foundation invested $2.2 million to create. It has been praised by Duncan as "the bible" for school restructuring. Duncan incorporated it into public policy, and reformers all around the country use it.[96]

In 2007, Gates and Broad declared that they were combining efforts and would invest $60 million dollars to get both the Democratic and Republican parties to consider their ideas for educational reform. The candidates responded, and addressed the topics of teacher merit pay and school reform. It was the appointment of Arne Duncan, former CEO of Chicago schools that made the foundations happy. It did not take Duncan long to replace many key players of his staff with members of school management organizations, training programs, think tanks and advocacy groups of the Gates and Broad Foundations. Soon after, the RTT initiative, which was the first time that states had to enter a competition for money. In order to apply, states had to write a roughly 350-page proposal, and the Department of Education outlined strict key requirements. For example, if in their proposal, a state did not include student test scores as part of teacher evaluations, they would not even be allowed to apply. Many of the requirements meant that some states had to rewrite laws that allowed for more charters and made it easier for merit pay to be introduced into school districts.

The Gates Foundation was there to help if a state had difficulties writing the proposal. In 2009, they picked fifteen applicants, and offered them each $250,000 dollars to hire consultants to write their proposals. Gates was anxious to have more districts with which to experiment. Money makes all of this possible, and even makes it possible to infiltrate news programs that impart information to the public. In 2010, both Gates and Broad financed *NBC News Education Nation,* which was a series of programs on our nation's education system that aired on several networks, including *Today* and *Nightly News.* The programs were criticized as weighing heavily on Duncan's and the foundations' agendas. Should wealthy private foundations be deciding public policy for public schools?

Chapter Seven

PHILADELPHIA
SCHOOLS TODAY

W hen Arlene Ackerman started as superintendent of
the Philadelphia School District in 2008, she was a
controversial figure from the beginning. She had served as
superintendent in both San Francisco and Washington, DC, where she
had contentious relationships with many public figures and politicians.
Many Philadelphians were outraged when it was revealed that she was
hired at an annual base salary of $325,000 (not including perks, benefits,
and bonuses), approximately $150,000 more than the mayor of the city.
When she accepted the new position in Philadelphia, she inherited a
district in peril. According to an article by *Philadelphia Magazine*, "The
problem is that Philadelphia can't easily afford a short-timer right now.
Despite the gains made in the Vallas years (Paul Vallas was the former
superintendent who left the district with a $73 million dollar deficit), the
school district is still an embarrassment. A staggering 44 percent of our
city's kids drop out, with Latinos (59 percent) and African-Americans
(49 percent) leading the exodus. An April study showed the average
Philly dropout consumes $319,000 in social services over the course
of his lifetime. And a 2006 study revealed that roughly 80 percent of

the city's murderers *and* their victims are dropouts. More to the point, national research demonstrates that it takes schools CEOs six years to enact lasting benefits."[97]

At the beginning of her term, Ackerman expressed concern over the high attrition rate of teachers. According to a 2007 study by Research for Action, less than half of the teachers who were hired in 1999 were still employed in the district by the fall of 2002.[1] She pointed out that close to 1,000 teachers retired or resigned from the district, which negatively affected students because many ended up being taught by unqualified substitutes due to the shortage. When certified teachers are unavailable, substitutes, not certified in the class in which they are placed, act more like babysitters, sitting in on a class while students spend the class period socializing. Sometimes this goes on for months in classes where teachers cannot be found in a specific subject area. This cost months and months of wasted learning time. In September of 2008, on the school district website, it was announced that Ackerman was unveiling a forty-five-day action plan to address low achievement at eighty-five elementary, middle, and high schools. "The District named the participating schools "Empowerment Schools" to signify its commitment to providing the resources and supports the schools need to transform from under-performing into high-achieving learning environments." Schools were classified as Empowerment Schools if they had not attained Adequate Yearly Progress (AYP) targets under No Child Left Behind Act (NCLB), and were in what the district called, "Corrective Action Level II."[98]

Ackerman's plan focused on turning schools around through specific interventions, including support such as "increased resources, additional school personnel, and more support from the central offices." The empowerment schools, it was announced, would receive monthly walk-throughs, a parent ombudsman, a student advisor, a part-time retired principal, and an increased nursing staff, among other programs. Ackerman created fifteen "Empowerment Response Teams," responsible for overseeing the implementation of these programs. "We will know that we are making progress in turning these schools around when we see evidence of success measures that include improved attendance, increased school safety, increased parent involvement and the attainment of various academic benchmarks,"[99] the Superintendent said.

In the spring of 2009, Ackerman unveiled her five-year strategic plan, *Imagine 2014,* to change Philadelphia's most needy schools. She addressed the problem of failing schools with a turnaround plan for thirty-five low-performing schools, announcing proposals for drastic changes; including getting rid of bad teachers, extending the school day and implementing some kind of performance pay. The teacher's union expressed resistance to the idea of performance pay and a longer school day, but in the end, the Philadelphia School Reform Commission approved the plan with a first-year budget of $126 million dollars (the performance pay plan was not carried through). Ackerman's Renaissance Schools began in the fall of 2010. Having identified the chronically failing schools, Ackerman selected a number of them to be managed by the district, and others to be run by external organizations. The union was originally informed that fourteen schools would be "Renaissance-eligible," but that the School District intended to take on only three or four schools in the beginning. These three to four schools would follow the "Promise Academy" model, and would be run by the School District, not by charter schools. Ackerman ended up choosing to take over all fourteen schools. Five of them were made into Promise Academies, with new administrations and teachers, and more flexibility in school programs, and would be under Ackerman's control, employing the union's teachers. It was announced that the other nine would be outsourced to "turnaround teams" —charter companies.

Most charter schools do not have teachers unions, which is the main reason that many district teachers choose not to apply. Teachers in Philadelphia have experienced too many injustices on the job, and fear the lack of accountability in charter schools. Jerry Jordan, the head of the PFT Philadelphia Federation of Teachers (PFT) expressed a concern about losing so many teachers, and said that if he had known his union would take such a big hit, he would never have negotiated the labor agreement in January 2010.

Advocates of charter schools in Pennsylvania were happy to see the shift of thousands of students away from the district. In thirteen years, the charter school movement in Philadelphia has grown from zero to sixty-seven schools and more than 36,000 students, supported by a large political base and financed by $400 million in taxpayer dollars. Charter schools have now been around long enough to be able to document several failures and scandals of their own. The day before Ackerman released her decision on the fourteen Renaissance schools, an audit of charter schools was released, and many examples of mismanagement and shady practices were revealed. Many charter schools in Philadelphia have been run by private companies that have no experience in education. "It hardly seems like this is the time to rush forward into new charter schools," PFT president Jerry Jordan commented. "First, we should spend some time learning how to control the ones we've got. Instead of making neighborhood schools a lifeline for disadvantaged students and a beacon of hope in struggling communities, the district is once again auctioning them off to the highest bidders."[100]

In 2010, Ackerman allowed seven of Philadelphia's toughest, failing schools to be managed by charter schools. The school's new private managers included Universal Companies, ASPIRA of Pennsylvania, Mastery Charter Schools, and Scholar Academies. In the spring of 2011, she turned over six more schools to private companies, including three high schools. Many parents and teachers have pushed to keep the children in their own neighborhoods and the Philadelphia School District has been adamant about creating neighborhood schools so that children could attend schools close to home. Some charter schools, such as Mastery, have been established in former district buildings, but allow students to come from all over the city. Some charters have demonstrated improvements, but many have not been able to prove changes in student achievement. Mastery Charter Schools now runs ten schools in Philadelphia, but there have been rumors that their success is due to "counseling out" bad students.

In the spring of 2011, just six months into the first year of the Promise Academies, we heard rumors of budget cuts. By April it became a reality, when the district announced that due to Pennsylvania's Republican Governor Tom Corbett's 2011–2012 budget, which cut education money by $1.2 billion dollars, Philadelphia schools faced a shortfall of $629 million dollars. It was spring, and suddenly teachers were now facing layoffs. Teachers had signed a two-year contract, which was now null. Teachers scrambled to send out resumes and interview at other schools. What our principal and superintendent had referred to as "the Promise Academy movement" began to crumble around us, and teachers and students alike began to question its validity. All of a sudden, after six months of team teaching, longer days and Saturday school, the district started talking about teacher lay-offs, larger class sizes, firing art, and music teachers, replacing full day kindergarten with a half-day program, and firing 3,820 district employees. The TransPass program, which provided 45,000 students with bus passes to ride city busses to get to school, was also in danger of being cut. Teachers, parents, and students began to protest in front of school district headquarters, and all over the city.

Ackerman had received federal stimulus money to start her "Renaissance Program," and many began to question her management abilities, "Hadn't she known that the money would only last a certain time period? Why hadn't she budgeted the money better?" She had used a huge portion of the money to hire an additional 1,200 employees, and now they would be laid off. Needless to say, there was a lot of anger towards the superintendent, and many started to refer to her as "Queen Arlene." The additional funding also paid for longer school days, summer programs, and Saturday programs. Teachers admitted that the Saturday program was a bust and a waste of money, since teachers were paid, schools were open, but because students could not be required to attend, only less than one third of students showed up, and little learning went on. A lot of money was wasted.

The next controversy came late in the year when the School Reform Commission discussed the possibility of protecting Promise Academy teachers from layoffs, because we had signed a contract that was supposed to protect us for two years. Non-Promise Academy teachers protested this idea, and in the end, it was rejected. About 1,500 teachers were laid off. It was a difficult summer for the district. In August 2011, after all of the layoffs, there were 1,335 teacher vacancies. At the end of the summer, 325 teachers were called back. I ended up going to a different Promise Academy in another part of the city. However, with little money to work with, the only change was the new moniker, new uniforms, and different teachers. The children came to school with the same problems every day. There was no more funding for special services. Because of the loss of money, Saturday school was cut, and the extra school hour from 3 to 4 PM was reduced to four days a week. Essentially, this extra hour was the only visible change that remained. New teachers had been hired, but they were hired from other schools around the city. A shifting of an educational team with no new training for teachers, no funds for special services to offer the students meant that little change could take place. Several months into the year, the principal announced that the budget had dried up, police officers were laid off, attendance was low, and violent incidents were back up.

Ackerman stayed in Philadelphia for three years, when after much criticism from the public, she resigned in 2011.

In addition to the budget woes, Ackerman was also involved in several other controversies. She lost the confidence of many when in September 2010, it was revealed that she took a contract away from a company that had already begun to install surveillance cameras in nineteen schools classified by the state as "persistently dangerous." She then gave the contract to a African American owned company, IBS Communications Inc., which was awarded a $7.5 million emergency, no-bid security contract. IBS was not on a state-approved list of contractors eligible for emergency work. According to the Philadelphia Inquirer, Ackerman later told several managers that "she was sick of the school district giving work to white contractors who "do not look like [her] and Lee [Nunnery],"[101] her deputy at the time. Ackerman and Nunnery are African American.

Ackerman also drew criticism when in December of 2009, violent attacks against Asian students occurred at South Philadelphia High School. Up to thirty students were violently beat up, when groups of African American students ran up and down the halls, invading classrooms and randomly attacking the Asian students. Feeling unsafe at school, many Asian students boycotted classes for a week afterwards. They complained that staff members did not intervene, and they were afraid to walk to the bus and subway stops after school. They asked the superintendent to meet with them to address these serious incidents. Ackerman refused for weeks to meet with them, and focused on her reasoning behind the attacks, blaming the issue on what she said was "retaliation" against some Asian students who had attacked an African American student in school earlier in the year. She then appointed a group of mostly African American students, who were not involved in the attacks, as "student ambassadors" to discuss solutions to the problem. She also said that schools were being expected to solve societal problems, and blamed the problem on the media, and on the advocacy groups who were supporting the Asian students.

A meeting was called in January, and Ackerman invited her ambassadors, but not the Asian victims, who were understandably upset for her lack of support. She commented through her spokesperson that she was very busy with other more pressing issues, such as the district budget. Needless to say, she angered many parents and students who feared coming to school each day.

In February of 2011, Ackerman was involved in yet another problem when a school in South Philly was slated to be converted into a Promise Academy. Audenried High School, located in one of the poorest, most violent areas of the city, had been referred to as the

"Prison on the Hill" for years, and had a history of problems. Even though the school had been completely rebuilt into a $55 million facility, it was still not performing up to the state standards, and Ackerman decided that it would have to be overhauled and would be part of her "Renaissance School" initiative. It was ultimately decided that the school would be run by Universal Companies, a private organization that had run several elementary charter schools, and was interested in taking over the high school as well. Universal had been awarded a $500,000 federal planning grant to turn around the poor surrounding neighborhoods. They also planned to eventually convert the neighborhood into "Promise Neighborhoods." It was announced in 2011 that based on student enrollment, Universal would receive up to $9 million in charter school payments to run Audenried and Vare Middle School. The teachers in the existing school would be force-transferred to other schools across the district. Though they would be given a chance to re-apply for their jobs, only 50 percent of them could ultimately be rehired.

One teacher, Hope Moffett, who had taught English at Audenried for three years, was upset over Ackerman's decision. She had been working tirelessly to prepare her students for PSSAs (the state tests). But before they even got a chance to take the tests, the district announced that the school would be turned into a Renaissance school. Moffett stated, "The District told us that if we implemented all of their interventions, we wouldn't become a Renaissance school. I feel like I've lied to my students because I believed something that wasn't true."[102] She felt that there was a lack of transparency; the district was not backing up their claims with data, and that by all indications, the school should have made AYP that year. Because Moffett led class discussions about the district plans for the school, and was outspoken about the district's decision, she faced disciplinary action. At a district informational meeting on February 9, 2011, Moffett spoke up and voiced her concerns about the impact of turning Audenried into a Renaissance school. After the meeting, a group of community members and students planned a protest for the next week. Even though she was not directly involved in the organization of the protest, she did assign an essay to her English student based on the controversy. She also lent bus tokens to some of her students to attend the protest. Soon after, Moffett received a letter from the district, ordering her to report to a room in a basement of the District's High School Academic Division, otherwise known as "the rubber room" or "teacher's jail," instead of her classroom. She also received a gag letter from the District, ordering her to refrain from speaking publicly about the incident, and threatening further disciplinary action if she did not follow the directive.

At the beginning of March 2011, the district sent a letter to Moffett informing her of their intention to fire her. It was based on the fact that she gave the students bus tokens to leave school to attend a protest against the superintendent's decision to convert Audenried into a charter school, "endangering the welfare of children." [103] Jerry Jordan president of the Philadelphia Federation of Teachers (the teacher's union), vowed to fight the decision, "I am outraged that the district has given Hope Moffett notice of their intent to terminate her. The charges are ridiculous, and the PFT will fight to restore Hope to her teaching position and defend her for exercising her First Amendment rights."

The PFT went to federal court to file a legal complaint on Moffett's behalf. Jordan called for a mass demonstration of teachers, and stated to the press, "Hope is just one of the many. The suit is being filed on behalf of all PFT members to protect their rights to speak freely, without fear of retaliation or intimidation by the district. My members are very concerned about freedom of speech, what's happening in their schools, and the lack of professional treatment they are receiving. They want an action to voice their sentiments." Removing a teacher from the classroom usually only occurs when there is violence or physical misconduct, and much attention was given to the fact that high-ranking administrators were involved in her first conference. Many felt that Moffett's assignment to the rubber room was retaliatory and intimidating, and that the issue was receiving more attention because Moffett's comments were directed at the superintendent. Before her investigatory conference, Moffett provided a copy of her letter from the district to the publication, *The Notebook*, which published its contents, after she had received notice not to disclose any information to the public.

Soon after the teacher demonstration to support Moffett, which drew over 1,000 Philadelphia teachers in front of the district headquarters in protest, Ackerman spoke out. "We believe that Ms. Moffett in her zeal to help children understand that they have a right to protest, we believe that she crossed the line." When asked if she thought that the protests were driven by teachers, she answered, "Absolutely. Because you know what? When we give the parents the data, when we show the parents what it can be, there's a whole different conversation that happens. When we hear what the conversation is about, it's not about, "how can we change the school so these young people can get a better education? It's about 'We're making progress, or I want to stay here with my students." I am totally focused on these young people, and I am not going to let adults who have their personal agendas get in the way of what I am trying to do."[104] Ackerman seemed to believe that when teachers care about their students they have "personal agendas," but when she "cared" it had a more noble meaning.

In late March, it was announced that Moffett would not be fired after all. The district decided to back down from its initial plan to terminate her, and that they would allow her to return to the classroom. Many still believe that in spite of the district's insistence about its concern for the safety of the students, the real reason for Moffett's removal and threat of termination was an attempt to silence a vocal critic of its controversial plan to hand Audenried over to Universal Companies, who would convert it into a charter school. Ultimately, in the fall of 2011, Universal did open the school under the new name, Universal Audenried Charter High School. "This settlement reinforces our belief that PFT members have the right to voice their concerns about workplace issues without threat of retribution or intimidation from their employer,"[105] PFT president Jerry Jordan said in a statement.

After much public discussion, in August of 2011, Ackerman finally quit as the Superintendent of the Philadelphia School District. During her more than three years in Philly, she had clashed with city officials, teachers and parents. She will most likely be remembered more for the controversy she caused than for her achievements. Up until the moment she boarded the plane to New Mexico, where she retired, she was creating headlines. After months of insisting that she would not leave, in the end, Ackerman received $905,000 plus $86,000 in unused vacation pay as a settlement package. She was paid $905,000 to walk away from her job. $405,000 came from anonymous donors, the rest from taxpayer dollars. She was criticized for her mismanagement of funds and poor management of employees. The district's $664 million budget gap this year, which was due in large part to huge cuts in state and federal aid, led to thousands of pink slips, and program cuts. She was replaced temporarily by her deputy superintendent, until a new superintendent could be found. In her last bold move, several weeks after she packed up her office, Ackerman applied for unemployment. The state ultimately denied her claim.

In January 2012, Thomas Knudsen, a financial turnaround specialist, was hired as the District's Chief Recovery Officer. His job was to analyze the district budget, and close a $61 million shortfall. After several months of analysis, the district announced the bad news in the spring of 2012. A statement was released that indicated that sixty-four schools could be closed over the next five years, and hundreds of central office jobs could be eliminated. A reorganization proposal revealed more than half a billion dollars in budget cuts in the district by 2017. The plan includes dividing the remaining schools into "achievement networks," which would be run by teams of educators or non-profit organizations (charter schools). Each achievement network could have up to twenty to thirty schools, and would be created based on either a common geography or educational philosophy. The district predicts that by 2017, 40 percent of the students in the district will be attending charter schools. The remaining 60 percent will most likely be the poorest of the poor, children whose parents are not equipped to be involved in their children's education, do not make choices about their children's schools, enroll their children in the nearest neighborhood schools, and let the schools take it from there. These are the parents whose attitudes are "Just getta 'D,' woudja?" These children will be left in public schools that run on bare bones budgets, and the future does not look bright. These schools need more funding, because they are trying to educate children who need additional services. Many of these children have great potential, just as those children whose parents make choices. Unfortunately, the government, whether state or federal, fails to support them.

When Pennsylvania's governor Tom Corbett announced his state budget for 2011-2012, it included "total statewide PreK-12 cuts to education of $1.18 billion, which was a 15percent total cut. The biggest cut in state funding was for basic education, which was cut statewide by $550 million. The budget completely eliminated many important education programs that had benefitted disadvantaged students and schools, such as:

- Accountability Grants (at-risk student tutoring; PreK; kindergarten): $259 million cut
- Reimbursing School Districts for Charter Schools: $224 million cut
- Education Assistance Program (at-risk student tutoring): $47.6 million cut
- School Improvement Grants: $10.8 million cut
- High School Reform: $1.8 million cut[106]

At a speech to the American Federation for Children in Washington, DC, the governor explained his support of competition in public education, and of vouchers as a solution to poverty and failing schools, "For many children, a zip code sentences them to a second-rate education. That can change with something as simple as competition."

He then goes on to describe a school in Harrisburg called the Nativity School that has accepted young people from other schools. "Some of those children enter as sixth graders who read on a second-grade level. By eighth grade, they are reading at eighth-grade level or better ...it is being done by flesh-and-bone teachers and it is being done because they are not there for job security. They are not there for the money." Corbett implies that private school teachers teach out of the goodness of their hearts and public school teachers teach for the money.

According to their website, the Nativity School is "a privately run, independent, non-denominational, faith-based preparatory middle school." I have no doubt that this school is doing great work. But Governor Corbett believes in vouchers, giving a check to parents and allowing them to take it to charters or private schools, to escape the horrible conditions of public schools. Corbett goes on to say, "I could tell you a similar story about a charter school in York County. And I could tell you endless stories about the religious and private schools across the state ... where a child-centered, values-oriented education makes the difference." Corbett wants to support private schools and charter schools, and believes that this will make public schools more competitive, while at the same time cutting their funding. Corbett believes that students are leaving public schools because they are looking for something better, and "to make them stay, the public school must offer them something better. The school must compete."[107] Somehow, they must do it with less money.

Corbett explains, "The only way I see to create that competition, to create that student mobility, is to make the funding portable. I liken it to a backpack: a family is allotted money for their child's education. It doesn't start at the school. It's carried to the school with that child. And each school competes to attract—or retain—that child. There is no way to separate funding from the reform. Not when competition is the agent of change. And, after decades of watching our leaders try everything else, the only effective change-maker I can name is competition. Failing schools must be helped to find new ways to improve and implement turn-around models. Competition does that." He then states, "It also seems to sort out the students who really want to break loose." So what about the students who can't break loose? What about the kids who want to learn, but have no parental support? What about the students who live on friends' couches, whose parents are addicts, are unemployed, and who have no one to advocate for them?

The new school district plan is based on giving parents more choice. Parents who vocalize their concerns want smaller class sizes, libraries, adequate security, music and art teachers, which are programs that are not included in the district's new plan. Thomas Knudsen, Chief Recovery Officer explained that the financial future of the budget was still unclear, due to the fact that the originally projected shortfall of $186 million had grown to $218 million (as of April 2012). The district plan will support high performing schools, closing low-performing ones and supporting growth of charter schools.

The recent district decisions reflect a continuing trend in public divestment in education. In an interview with Professor James Lytle, of Pennsylvania State University's Graduate School of Education, he stated, "I think we are in the early stages of the dissolution of conventional schooling." When asked if he thought that the drastic changes to our education system meant an educational/economic hierarchy, he answered, "That's a rhetorical question, but the answer is 'yes.' And, it really is problematic when you think that, historically, providing equal opportunity has been the role of public schools in America. … I think what you are seeing, and not just in Pennsylvania, is a reduction in the commitment to urban and rural public schooling. … I have yet to meet anybody who thinks there will be a major reinvestment in urban public schools anytime soon. The thinking behind the market approach is that you reward success and you punish failure. So if schools aren't performing, you close them, which is ostensibly how markets work. But commentators remind us that when auto companies and Wall Street collapsed, not a lot of people got punished. Yet in public education, low-performing schools are getting hammered, and the schools that are most affected are schools that serve poor and minority kids. And lurking in the shadows are the Gates Foundation, the Walton Foundation, and other high-influence individuals and organizations that have no public accountability, but are supporting market-driven solutions as the way to improve education in the U.S.—despite the fact that there is no research evidence that supports this 'solution.'"[108]

In June of 2012, it was announced that Dr. William R. Hite Jr. would be the new superintendent of the Philadelphia School District. He came from Prince George's County Public Schools in Maryland, where he had worked as the superintendent since 2009. Since the spring, when the news had surfaced of the impending school closures, we knew that the confirmation and details were coming before the end of the year. On December 12, the list of schools to be closed was released: thirty-seven schools were slated for closure, including twenty-two elementary schools, four middle schools, and eleven high schools, of which Vaux High School was one. There would also be program mergers between schools, and several schools would be relocated to consolidate and save on space. All told, over 17,000 students and 2,000 staff would be affected. The district announced that there would not be any teacher layoffs, but other jobs could be lost, including administrative and support positions. It was announced that the closures would be effective June 30, 2013. The superintendent reported that the district had borrowed $300 million to pay its bills through the end of the school year, and estimated that the closings would save approximately $28 million.

On December 20, hundreds of protestors took to the streets in Center City to voice their opposition to the closures. At a meeting with the School Reform commission, "Theodore Yale, a teacher at the Philadelphia Military Academy at Elverson, a North Philadelphia school that would be combined with another military school and relocated at the current Roosevelt Middle School building in East Germantown, said that students would leave in droves if forced to make an hour-long commute on public transportation.

"I will not accept that losing scores of our best students to a system of charter schools that is already bleeding us dry is the only option," Yale said. "I will not accept that destroying one of the best schools in this jacked-up district is the only option."[109] Parents, teachers, and students expressed anger and sadness that their schools would be closed. Some fear that violence in the schools could worsen, as some schools will grow larger as they are forced to take in students from closed schools. Young children will have to travel further distances when their neighborhood schools are closed. Because Philadelphia is known for its neighborhood rivalries, some fear trouble when many students from those varying groups could be forced to cross the turf of their rivals and attend school with them. "I think it's definitely going to have an impact on safety. How significant, I can't say at this point," said Kelley B. Hodge, the state-appointed safe schools advocate, who helps victims of violence in Philadelphia's schools. "It's a very intense social experiment. I think every student in the district is going to be affected in some way, shape or fashion."[110]

Superintendent Hite explained to the public that by closing and consolidating schools, the district would be able to eliminate the underutilization of school buildings whose enrollment has decreased in the last few years. Parents and community activists, including the Philadelphia Coalition Advocating for Public Schools, have been trying to get the public involved in supporting the cause of saving Philadelphia's public schools. They believe that the district has a responsibility to listen to the concerned parents, and to take into consideration their misgivings about the drastic decision to close schools. The School District of Philadelphia has gone through extreme restructuring in the last few years, and the bottom line today is that there is little money to support the cost of educating our students. (On March 7, 2013, The Philadelphia Reform Commission voted to only close 23 schools).

Unfortunately, there are no easy solutions to the problems that our public schools face today. Much of the ideas of today's reformers involve tearing down teachers, creating even more high stakes testing, and funding charter and online schools for the select few, while ignoring the poor children who cannot access resources. There are huge numbers of poor children in inner cities who go to school each day without the tools they need to be successful. As a teacher in inner-city schools, it is my belief that we need to design schools that deal with the challenges of poverty head on. Schools need teams of professionals who can help with the psychological and emotional needs of children in poverty, to support them and guide them to become successful students and to go on to lead productive lives.

But in the meantime, life goes on as usual. One day this year, as I was getting ready to leave school for the day, I received a text from a friend asking if I had heard about the shooting in the Philadelphia subway, because it had happened on the same line I take every day to school. Earlier that day, students were heading home on the subway from several different schools in North Philadelphia. Apparently a fight broke out, and a 15-year-old boy stepped off the train, walked to the next set of doors and opened fire into the subway car, which was crowded with students. A seventeen-year-old was hit in the arm and a fourteen-year-old was hit in the leg.

The fifteen-year-old, who fired the shots, had attended Gratz High School in North Philly the previous year. He had since transferred to a different high school in Upper Darby, a township that borders the city. The previous day, he had been suspended for marijuana possession at the school. The school had recently found out that he had lied to get into the school, and he was about to be expelled. On the day of the suspension, he put his gun in his pocket and headed north on the subway to look for trouble. His parents turned him in to the police that evening. Today he sits in jail awaiting trial, where he will be tried as an adult, charged with attempted murder, aggravated assault, reckless endangerment, burglary, trespassing, and gun possession.

ACKNOWLEDGMENTS

I would like to thank my editor, for her support, guidance and patience. I would also like to give thanks to my publishing team at Morgan James for taking on the project and allowing me to tell this story. A special thanks to all of the hard working public school teachers across the country for their dedication, perseverance and commitment to the children every day in the classroom.

ABOUT THE AUTHOR

Louise Marr has been a public school teacher for over eleven years, both on the West and East Coasts. She has a Master of Education degree as well as a Master in Literature. She attended public schools, and all three of her children did as well. She teaches at a public high school in Philadelphia.

ENDNOTES

1   All names of the students in this book have been changed to protect their identities.

2   "Comprehensive Student Assistance Process," http://webgui.phila. k12.pa.us/offices/s/oss/programs--services/csap, accessed August 1, 2012.

3   "Assault on Learning," *Philadelphia Inquirer*, http://www.philly. com/philly/news/special_packages/inquirer/school-violence, accessed August 15, 2012.

4   "A Chance for Every Child," www.mittromney.com, accessed July 16, 2012, p. 8.

5   "A Chance for Every Child," www.mittromney.com, accessed July 16, 2012, p. 7.

6   Laura Pappano, *Inside School Turnarounds* (Cambridge: Harvard Education Press, 2010), 3.

7   Laura Pappano, *Inside School Turnarounds* (Cambridge: Harvard Education Press, 2010), 10.

8   Anthony Cody, "The Bad Teacher Bogeyman and Its Consequences," http://voices.washingtonpost.com/answer-sheet/anthony-cody/the-bad-teacher-bogeyman-and-w.html, accessed July 29, 2012.

9   Jay McCleod, *Ain't No Makin' It* (Boulder: Westview Press, 2009), 4–5.

10   "Guest Blog: Serve the Community, Serve the Students," A Broad View: The Official Blog of the School District of Philadelphia, http://www.phillyeducationblog.com/2011/03/guest-blog-serve-community-serve.html, accessed July 5, 2012.

11   Elijah Anderson, *Code of the Street* (New York: W.W. Norton & Company, 1999), 147.

12   Daniel Denvir, "Avoiding the Subject," *Philadelphia City Paper,* http://www.citypaper.net/news/2011-10-20-philadelphia-schools-sex-education.html, accessed July 18, 2012.

13   Daniel Denvir, "Avoiding the Subject," *Philadelphia City Paper,* http://www.citypaper.net/news/2011-10-20-philadelphia-schools-sex-education.html, accessed July 18, 2012.

14   Jeff Williams, Sarah Tanner-Anderson, and Alaiyo Kiasi-Barnes, "A Conversation with U.S. Secretary of Education Arne Duncan: Learning from One Another," http://onlinedigitalpublishing.com, accessed July 29, 2012.

15   Eric Jensen, *Teaching with Poverty in Mind* (Alexandria: ASCD, 2009).

16   Eric Jensen, *Teaching with Poverty in Mind* (Alexandria: ASCD, 2009).

17   Jean Johnson, *What's Trust Got to Do with It* (San Francisco: Public Agenda, 2011).

18   The Arc, www.thearc.org.

19   The Philadelphia Public School Notebook, April 2010.

20   The Philadelphia Public School Notebook, April 2010.

21   Eric Jensen, *Teaching with Poverty in Mind* (Alexandria: ASCD, 2009), 9.

22 Elijah Anderson, *Code of the Street* (New York: W.W. Norton & Company, 1999), 149.

23 "Philadelphia 2011: The State of the City," Philadelphia Research Initiative, Pew Charitable Trust, http://www.pewtrusts.org/uploadedFiles/wwwpewtrustsorg/Reports/Philadelphia_Research_Initiative/Philadelphia-City-Data-Population-Demographics.pdf.

24 "Children's Exposure to Violence," http://www.childrensdatabank.org.

25 "Children's Exposure to Violence," http://www.childrensdatabank.org.

26 "Effects of Poverty, Hunger, Homelessness on Children and Youth,"American Psychological Association, www.apa.org.

27 "Assault on Learning," *Philadelphia Inquirer.*

28 "Assault on Learning," *Philadelphia Inquirer.*

29 "Assault on Learning," *Philadelphia Inquirer.*

30 "Assault on Learning," *Philadelphia Inquirer.*

31 Philadelphia School District Budgets, 2012.

32 Signithia Fordham and John Ogbu, "Black Students' School Success: Coping with the Burden of Acting White," *Urban Review* 18, no. 2 (1986), 177ff.

33 Signithia Fordham and John Ogbu, "Black Students' School Success: Coping with the Burden of Acting White," *Urban Review* 18, no. 2 (1986), 177ff.

34 Signithia Fordham and John Ogbu, "Black Students' School Success: Coping with the Burden of Acting White," *Urban Review* 18, no. 2 (1986), 177ff.

35 Source: http://www.education.state.pa.us.

36 "Learning Disabilities and Young Children: Identification and Intervention," http://www.ldonline.org/article.

37 National Joint Committee on Learning Disabilities, http://www.ncld.org.

38 "Learning Disabilities and Young Children: Identification and Intervention,"http:// www.ldonline.org/article.

39   Daniel Lyons, "Bill Gates and Randi Weingarten," *Newsweek*, December 20, 2010.

40   Diane Ravitch, "Why VAM Is Junk Science," Diane Ravitch's Blog, July 16, 2012.

41   Dan Mccaffrey, "Evaluating Value-Added Models for Teacher Accountability," Rand Coorperation, 2003.

42   Paul Socolar, "New Data, Same Staffing Inequities at High-Poverty Schools," *The Notebook* 16, no. 4 (Summer 2009).

43   Wendy Harris, "Where Have All the Teachers of Color Gone?" *The Notebook* 16, no. 4 (Summer 2009).

44   Laura Pappano, *Inside School Turnarounds* (Cambridge: Harvard Education Press, 2010), 103.

45   Paul Socolar, "New Data, Same Staffing Inequities at High-Poverty Schools," *The Notebook* 16, no. 4 (Summer 2009).

46   Paul Socolar, "New Data, Same Staffing Inequities at High-Poverty Schools," *The Notebook* 16, no. 4 (Summer 2009).

47   Stephanie Gaspary, "Creating a Great Place to Work: Lessons from 2010's FORTUNE 100 Best Companies to Work For," thehiringsite. careerbuilder.com/2010/06/30.

48   Jeff Williams, Sarah Tanner-Anderson, and Alaiyo Kiasi-Barnes, "A Conversation with U.S. Secretary of Education Arne Duncan: Learning from One Another," http://onlinedigitalpublishing.com, accessed July 29, 2012.

49   Lynnell Hancock, "Why Are Finland's Schools Successful?" Smithsonian.com, September 2011.

50   "The Finnish Education Model: Highlights, Resources, and Research," Excellence in K-12 Education: Experiences in Finland and Washington State, Economic Opportunities Institute, November 13, 2012, http://www.eoionline.org/education/reports/ FinnishResearchSummary-Nov12.pdf.

51   Pennsylvania Department of Education, http://www.education. state.pa.us.

52   Diane Ravitch, *Death and Life of the Great American School System* (New York: Basic Books, 2010), 103.

53   Mitt Romney, "A Chance for Every Child," www.mittromney.com, accessed July 16, 2012.

54   Daniel de Vise, "Bill Gates Talks about Teacher, Pay, Class Size," *Washington Post,* February 28, 2011.

55   Bill Gates, speech to American Federation of Teachers, July 10, 2010.

56   Bill Gates, speech to American Federation of Teachers, July 10, 2010.

57   Steven Brill, *Class Warfare* (New York: Simon and Schuster, 2011).

58   Kelly Ni, "Education Head Wants Prestige for Teachers," *The Epoch Times,* July 31, 2011.

59   "Transcript: Obama Speaks to the U.S. Hispanic Chamber of Commerce," 2007, *Washington Post,* http://www.washingtonpost. com/wp-srv/politics/documents/Obama_Hispanic_Chamber_ Commerce.html.

60   Source: www.ed.gov, accessed August 13, 2012.

61   Source: www.ed.gov, accessed August 13, 2012.

62   Center for Educator Compensation Reform, "New York City's School-Wide Performance Bonus Program," October 2010, http://www.cecr.ed.gov/pdfs/summaries/CECR_CS_NYC_ PerfBonusProgram.pdf.

63   Julie A. Marsh et al, *A Big Apple for Educators: New York's Experiment with School-Wide Performance Bonuses Final Education Report* (Santa Monica: Rand Corporation, 2011), http://www.rand.org/content/ dam/rand/pubs/monographs/2011/RAND_MG1114.pdf.

64   Mark Ambinder, "Obama Insists on Performance Standards for Teachers," *The Atlantic,* July 29, 2010.

65   Source: www.ed.gov, accessed September 1, 2012.

66   Andy Smarick, "Diplomatic Mission," *Education Next* 11, no. 1 (Winter 2011).

67 "Arne Duncan Talks Race to the Top, Teacher Support, and Pay," *Huffington Post*, February 17, 2012.

68 Julie A. Marsh et al, *A Big Apple for Educators: New York's Experiment with School-Wide Performance Bonuses Final Education Report* (Santa Monica: Rand Corporation, 2011), http://www.rand.org/content/dam/rand/pubs/monographs/2011/RAND_MG1114.pdf.

69 Stephanie Simon, Privatizing Public Schools: Big Firms Eyeing Profits from U.S. K-12 Market," *Huffington Post*, August 2, 2012.

70 Diane Ravitch, *Death and Life of the Great American School System* (New York: Basic Books, 2010).

71 Sam Dillon, "Behind Grass-Roots School Advocacy, Bill Gates," *New York Times*, May 21, 2011.

72 Sam Dillon, "Behind Grass-Roots School Advocacy, Bill Gates," *New York Times*, May 21, 2011.

73 Leonie Haimson, "The Most Dangerous Man in America," *Huffington Post*, February 17, 2012.

74 Steven Brill, *Class Warfare* (New York: Simon and Schuster, 2011), 116.

75 Steven Brill, *Class Warfare* (New York: Simon and Schuster, 2011), 116-117.

76 Source: www.k12.com.

77 Stephanie Saul, "Profits and Questions at Online Charter Schools," *New York Times*, December 12, 2011.

78 Source: www.k12.com.

79 Source: www.k12.com.

80 Grace Hood, "Overworked and Underpaid at COVA?" EdNews, March 19, 2012.

81 Stephanie Saul, "Profits and Questions at Online Charter Schools," *New York Times*, December 12, 2011.

82 Stephanie Saul, "Profits and Questions at Online Charter Schools," *New York Times*, December 12, 2011.

83 Source: www.publiccharters.org.

84   Steven Brill, *Class Warfare* (New York: Simon and Schuster, 2011), 144-145.

85   "The State of the New York Charter School Sector," New York Center for Charter Schools, 2012.

86   Michael Winerip, "Message from a Charter School: Thrive or Transfer," *New York Times*, July 10, 2010.

87   Elaine Allard, "ELLs Have Limited School Choices," *The Notebook*, Fall 2008.

88   Elaine Allard, "ELLs Have Limited School Choices," *The Notebook*, Fall 2008.

89   Source: credo.stanford.edu.

90   Dan Conway, "Waiting for Superman: American Liberalism Spearheads the Right Wing Attack on Public Education," October 7, 2009, World Socialist Web Site, http://www.wsws.org/en/articles/2010/10/wfsm-o07.html.

91   Dan Conway, "Waiting for Superman: American Liberalism Spearheads the Right Wing Attack on Public Education," October 7, 2009, World Socialist Web Site, http://www.wsws.org/en/articles/2010/10/wfsm-o07.html.

92   Source: hcz.org.

93   Source: www.state.nj.us.

94   Source: www.broadcenter.org/academy.

95   Jason Riley, "Was the $5 Billion Worth It?" *Wall Street Journal*, July 23, 2011.

96   John Thompson, "Does Bill Gates Owe Arne Duncan an Apology or Not?" *Huffington Post*, July 17, 2011.

97   Steve Volk, "Arlene Ackerman Profile: Queen Arlene," *Philadelphia Magazine*, January 2010.

98   Philadelphia School District website, www.phila.k12.pa.us.

99   Philadelphia School District website, www.phila.k12.pa.us.

100 Tony West, "Surprises and Questions Stalk Ackerman's 'Renaissance Schools," *The Public Record*, April 15, 2010.

101 Martha Woodall, "Former Philadelphia School Official Alleges He Was Fired for Whistle Blowing," *Philadelphia Inquirer,* March 5, 2012.

102 Benjamin Herold, "The Audacity of Hope Moffett," *The Notebook,* February 20, 2011.

103 Benjamin Herold, "District Exiles Outspoken Audenried Teacher," *The Notebook,* February 17, 2011.

104 Benjamin Herold, "A Conversation with Superintendent Arlene Ackerman," *Newsworks,* March 6, 2011.

105 Josh Cornfield, "Philadelphia Teacher Hope Moffett Wins Her First Amendment Lawsuit Against the Philadelphia School District," Parent Advocates.org, March 18, 2011.

106 Baruch Kintisch, "Key Facts about Governor Corbett's Education Budget for 2011-12," Education Law Center, www.elc-pa.org.

107 Governor Corbett, "Poor Need Education Escape Route," speech delivered May 22, 2011.

108 Tanya Barrientos, "Q & A with James H. Lyte," *Penn Current*, May 19, 2011.

109 Kristen A. Graham and Robert Moran, "Marchers Take Their Case to the SRC," *Philadelphia Inquirer,* December 21, 2012.

110 Susan Snyder and Dylan Purcell, "Closings May Worsen School Violence," *Philadelphia Inquirer,* December 14, 2012.